EDITOR
Samina Quraeshi

CONSULTING EDITOR
David Scobey, Director, Arts of Citizenship Program
University of Michigan Taubman College of Architecture

CONTRIBUTING EDITOR
Cassim Shepard

DESIGN
Ivonne de la Paz
Maribel Gonzalez

ART DIRECTOR
James Pittman

IN CONSULTATION WITH
Elizabeth Plater-Zyberk &
Dr. Jose Szapocznik

PUBLISHER
Spacemaker Press, LLC
James G. Trulove, Publisher
1250 28th Street, NW
Washington, DC 20007

ISBN: 0-9749632-2-4

Printed in China

First Printing, 2005

1 2 3 4 5 6/08 07 06 05

UNIVERSITY OF MIAMI PARTNERS
School of Architecture, Center for Urban & Community Design
School of Communication, Center for Advancement of Modern Media,
Department of Journalism & Photography
School of Medicine, Center for Family Studies
School of Law, Center for Ethics and Public Service
School of Arts & Sciences, Department of History, Department of Fine Arts
School of Education

COMMUNITY PARTNERS
City of Miami, Mayor Manuel Diaz, Commissioner Johnny Winton,
Jason Walker, Homer Whittaker
Miami-Dade County, Commissioner Jimmy Morales, Will Johnson
The Collins Center for Public Policy
Wind & Rain, Inc.
Cityzens
Coconut Grove Local Development Corp.
The Grove Tree-Man Trust
Theodore R. Gibson Memorial Fund, Inc.
Thelma Gibson Health Initiative
Coconut Grove Village West Homeowners & Tenants Association
Duany Plater-Zyberk & Company
Grovites United to Survive, Inc.
Coconut Grove Family & Youth Intervention Center
Coconut Grove Chamber of Commerce
Coconut Grove Village Council
Coconut Grove Collaborative
Ecunemical Network of Coconut Grove
Coconut Grove Cares, Inc.
Coconut Grove Crime Prevention Council
Virrick Park Committee

WITH SUPPORT FROM
The U.S. Department of Housing & Urban Development
John S. & James L. Knight Foundation
Henry R. Luce Foundation
National Council of Architectural Registration Boards
University of Miami

REIMAGINING WEST COCONUT GROVE
A University - Community Partnership

CONTENTS

Our mission is to foster an interdisciplinary program of research, education and outreach that supports the people, places and processes essential for creating and sustaining family-centered communities.

"Nobody can tell now, exactly, why Rome and Paris and London began, or what made them endure and grow great. It is as if there were places and times in which human activity becomes a whirlpool which gathers force not only from man's courage and ambitions and high hopes but from the very tides of disaster and human foolishness which otherwise disperse them. Such cities seem to grow in spite of people, by some power of the whirlpool itself, which puts to work good and bad, fineness and cheapness, everthing, so long as it has

fibre and force and the quality of aliveness that makes life. Something like that, it seems to me, has happened here in South Florida, under the sun and the hurricane, on sand and pineland between the changeless Everglades and the unchanging sea. Miami has been building itself with all the tough thrust and vigor of a tropic organism. I doubt if it will be complete or the whirlpool slack, in a long time because its strength is that nothing human is foreign to it, or will be."

Marjory Stoneman Douglas

HISTORIES

I like talking about Coconut Grove, because it's my birthplace…But it's always important to have history, and I think it's important to have it written at some point, … because we lose so much.

Thelma Anderson Gibson

I first thought that our project in Coconut Grove was going to be an exercise in documentary making and teamwork. However, after walking through the neighborhood, I realized this project was going to be about history, help and hope; the extraordinary history of the area, the need to help the community and the hope that so many different people have for a very unique area of Miami."

Corbett Compel

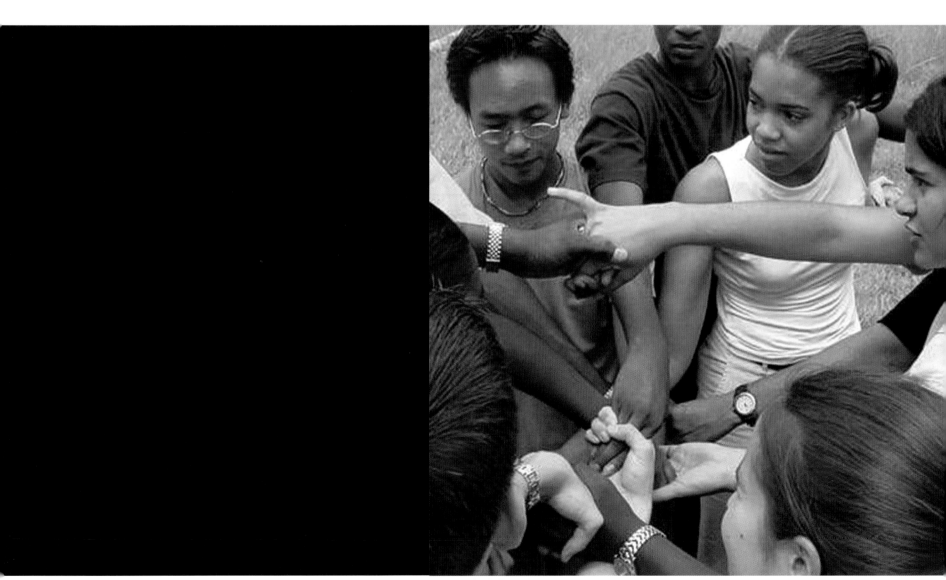

Photo: Richard Shepard

Introduction
**Interdisciplinary Community Building –
Strengthening a Neighborhood**

**Samina Quraeshi
Initiative for Urban and Social Ecology (INUSE)**

Authentic help means that all who are involved help each other mutually, growing together in common effort to understand the reality which they seek to transform. Only through such praxis — in which those who help and those who are being helped help each other simultaneously — can the act of helping become free from the distortion in which the helper dominates the helped.
—Paolo Friere, Pedagogy of the Oppressed

This collection of essays recounts recent efforts by the University of Miami and some of its community partners to devise an interdisciplinary approach to strengthening community in a distressed inner-city neighborhood. Specifically, it reflects the challenges and triumphs of the last five years of work by the Initiative for Urban and Social Ecology (INUSE) in the community of West Coconut Grove.

Located on the Miami-Coral Gables border between the University of Miami campus and the upscale shopping and entertainment areas of Coconut Grove to the east, West Coconut Grove is one of Miami's founding neighborhoods. Historically an Afro-Caribbean-American community, it includes among its residents sixth-generation descendants of Bahamians who settled in South Florida in the mid-1800s. Yet, despite this rich historical and cultural legacy, the history of the "West Grove" as a vital, thriving community lives only in the memories of its older residents, not in the reality they see before them. For the last forty years, the community has seen jobs decline and poverty rise as it has fought to retain its identity in the face of such social ills as poor health, drug abuse, and teenage pregnancy.

In stark contrast to surrounding areas where increased affluence has brought many positive changes, West Coconut Grove remains mired in poverty. More than 40 percent of its approximately 3,000 residents live under the poverty level: median household income is $14,191, compared to $47,506 in Coral Gables; and median income per capita is $10,308. Nearly 50 percent of the total population in West Coconut Grove is not employed or looking for work, and 50 percent of high-school students drop out without receiving a diploma. With such little economic opportunity, the problem of housing affordability is also acute.

So far, this historic enclave — roughly 65 blocks covering a half square mile — has been protected from gentrification by the density and stability of its ethnic population. The crime rate has also kept outside developers at bay; because of the high incidence of aggravated assaults

Photo: J.J. Gama-Lobo

and theft, people are reluctant to move into West Coconut Grove, and its long-time residents live in fear. However, without outside intervention or long-term goals for improvement, this important and unique Miami neighborhood will inevitably decline to the point where speculative development by outside forces will overwhelm the desires of existing residents and property owners. At that point its history and unique potential will be lost forever.

INUSE IN ACTION

To address this situation, the university has attempted to engage the challenges through its INUSE program, an innovative, interdisciplinary effort to serve as catalyst for physical and social change. INUSE reflects the view that the university, with its great wealth of resources, can be of great help to such communities. Reciprocally, the community can be of great service to the university as a site for research, planning and implementation of more effective social-development strategies. Furthermore, both can benefit from the process of collaboration itself.

The breakdown of community structures, the decline of social capital, and chronic poverty are not problems, however, that can be solved without serious commitment at street level. Thus, INUSE also reflects the view that the university must become less isolated from the world; it must roll up its sleeves and get its hands dirty. And if the university is to provide practical and participatory leadership in such places, it also must facilitate connections across disciplines. Thus, colleagues within the university must learn to cooperate and collaborate better.

These concerns have led to the framing of two main goals for INUSE activities:

The projects must redefine the relationship between the university and the community. This means establishing effective university–community partnerships, encouraging creative collaborative programs, incorporating education into community development, and enlisting the assistance of funders who support these aims. The projects must encourage new educational approaches within the university itself. This means promoting collaborations among existing university–community learning efforts scattered within the institution; and it means fostering new interdisciplinary teaching and learning arrangements to enhance critical thinking.

In pursuit of these goals, INUSE has worked to develop creative ways to serve West Coconut Grove. These essays tell the story of how. As outlined above, our view is that the university and the community can work together to advance community goals and enrich the student-faculty educational experience. However, inclusive decision-making in a community project is a complex challenge. There must be a common understanding and philosophy; but community leaders and university representatives must also listen for divergent themes so they can help each other understand positive approaches to real needs.

Instead of forcing solutions on the community, INUSE has sought to structure its initiatives to reinforce the efficacy of local institutions where community consensus is still intact, and provide the foundation for the building of a more focused, incremental and ongoing vision. As part of this effort, INUSE has tried to create (or reinforce) a positive new sense of place through a layering of actions, large and small, short- and long-term, by many different people who may either live, work or simply pass through the area.

Our efforts to promote social, economic and physical renaissance in West Coconut Grove have also tried to restore a strong, seamless fabric of social connectedness. This is the real glue that sustains families and promotes community. However, restoring a sense of common future involves reacquainting residents with the history of their place. Such shared awareness is essential to building trust, encouraging dialogue, and fostering more collaborative and constructive initiatives.

Part of our effort has also been to bolster the institutional capacity of our community partners and help them explore new avenues for collaboration with other organizations dedicated to community development.

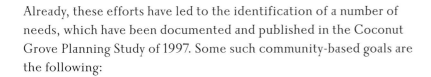
Photos: University of Miami Photography students

Already, these efforts have led to the identification of a number of needs, which have been documented and published in the Coconut Grove Planning Study of 1997. Some such community-based goals are the following:

• Improve Grand Avenue as a public, commercial street.
• Find viable businesses to operate in existing abandoned storefronts.
• Increase the rate of homeownership in the community, including scattered site infill buildings.
• Increase neighborhood efficacy and social capacity by convening property owners to consolidate fragmented improvement efforts.
• Improve public spaces (e.g. paving, landscaping, lighting and street furniture) to encourage private investment.
• Devise a strategic vision to ensure ongoing integrity of community.

STUDENT PARTICIPATION

One of the great resources available to a university-community initiative is the idealism and energy of students. In total, 272 students and 40 faculty members have been involved to date in the effort to catalyze long-term change in the West Grove and equip its residents with new knowledge and skills. These students and faculty have come from the Schools of Architecture, Law, Medicine, Nursing and Communication, and in the School of Arts and Sciences, from the Departments of History, Fine Arts, and Art History.

INUSE offers students a learning experience that is truly multifaceted. It emphasizes the need to explore problems from a variety of viewpoints, share knowledge, and consider a range of possible solutions.

INUSE's work in the West Grove follows several basic principles.

Cross-disciplinary learning. The interconnected nature of real-world issues calls for integrated approaches to learning and problem solving. Within the university, cooperating departments have opened courses to students and guest faculty from other fields related to the community's needs.

Service. INUSE provides students the chance to engage in fieldwork, applied research, and study within an overall ethic of community service. Students from different disciplines work directly with community partners so that applied learning may be a complement to academic coursework.

Real projects. Community and university partners work together to design place-based projects that are feasible and mutually supportive. Potential projects are evaluated for their ability to produce lasting results and inform and support future projects. Past and ongoing project have included the following:

• Building affordable homes on infill sites.
• Renovating business properties.
• Facilitating neighborhood planning for new community schools and health facilities.
• Identifying discrepancies in zoning and platting that discourage investment, and working with the city and county to remedy them.
• Working with Miami-Dade County to establish a One-Stop Welfare-to-Work Center.
• Facilitating provision of legal assistance for neighborhood residents.

- Establishing a K-8 neighborhood elementary charter school. [1]
- Creating a Community Resource Center that coordinates existing and new community-improvement efforts.
- Building six affordable homes for first-time homebuyers.
- Renovating a mixed-use building on Grand Avenue for occupation by businesses and tenants.
- Establishing three new local businesses in renovated stores.
- Improving access to community healthcare, social, legal and design services.
- Providing a neutral place for community discussion to take place.

What follows is a testament to some of these projects. For us, fostering a sense of place involves investigating a place's history, documenting its dynamics through visual and textual portraits of a community, mapping its assets and challenges towards coordinating a set of service-based interventions, and, finally, assessing what was done right and wrong and applying these lessons to future work.

Histories. West Grove's heritage is one of hard work and honorable gains, of strife as well as harmony. One necessary step in fostering a sense of community is to give voice to this shared history and its complex nuances. To help residents better understand their community's heritage, students in Professor Gregory Bush's class recorded and transcribed the oral histories and current viewpoints of community residents. These perspectives have become the foundation for an ongoing dialogue about the West Grove whose aim is to promote a richer understanding and deeper commitment to the community.

Two historians have also examined aspects of the West Grove-university relationship through targeted research work. Community historian Arva Moore Parks explored the challenges facing West Coconut Grove from its earliest days to the present in her essay, "History of West Coconut Grove in the Context of Miami." Meanwhile, Professor Robin Bachin considered the cycles of engagement and disengagement between universities and communities in general in her essay "Historical Changes in the Planning Process: The Role of Academics in Understanding Urbanism and Building Bridges with Community."

Portraits of a Community. Students in photography, film and multimedia have documented the interconnecting and sometimes conflicting layers of West Coconut Grove's physical and social fabric. Their record carries no assumptions of what should or could be. Professors Michael Carlebach, Lelen Bourgoignie, and Sanjeev Chatterjee have also documented the community's complex and rich imagery in their own work. Their visual archive of existing built forms is a complement to the digital presentations of students in classes taught by Professor David Burnett. These images are supported by reflections from residents and community leaders, including testimonies from Yvonne McDonald and Will Johnson.

Interventions. To date, INUSE has involved a wide range of partners from within the university: the Center for Urban and Community Design (architecture and design), the Center for Family Studies (social and behavioral sciences), the Institute for Public History (history), the Center for the Advancement of Modern Media (communications), the Department of Art and Art History (art), the Center for Ethics and Public Service (community legal services), and CITYZENS (a student-initiated design education project). These coordinated university-led efforts could not have fostered any significant change without parallel contributions by other institutions and individuals, from educators like Jennifer Jones to community organizers like Daniella Levine to socially conscious property developers like Andy Parrish. For all of us, the process became as much about the very nature of broad-based interdisciplinary collaboration as about the community-centered mission that inspired us to work together.

Educational interventions provide insight into strategies for enlisting young people in the collaborative process of community-building. Jennifer Jones' "Celebrating Children and the Arts" testifies to the dream that the Theodore R. and Thelma A. Gibson School has realized.

The use of design as a curricular tool to inspire youth to engage with their environment is the basis of the CITYZENS project. And educa-

The images in "The Tables are Turned" are stills from a documentary produced by students in Sanjeev Chatterjee's Advanced Electronic Media Production course.

tional policy initiatives, such as those discussed by Dr. Etiony Aldarando and Ms. Lisa Martinez, demonstrate the scope and potential of youth development programs. Incorporating young citizens is crucial to any hope for promoting a sustainable model of community involvement.

Daniella Levine shares her infectious passion while providing a powerful reminder of the need for community organization from within. Her challenge to community-builders to focus on prosperity rather than poverty compliments the projects outlined in the following piece, where architecture students have encouraged the citizens of West Coconut Grove to become agents of change in their own right. Students have proposed designs for schools and housing that resonate with the residents' heritage, culture and everyday needs. And all stakeholders have contributed to the Vision Plan, discussed here by Professors Richard Shepard and Eric Vogt.

Coursework under the direction of Professor Shepard has focused on designing and building affordable houses, one of which has been constructed and occupied. This feat would not have been possible without the commitment of a visionary local development firm, Wind and Rain. Director Andy Parrish shares some of the lessons of Wind and Rain's experience in his essay, "Learning Right from Wrong."

Behavioral and social psychology students from the School of Medicine have counseled families and children (in the process, saving lives and building futures), and worked with teachers, housing officials, police, and social-service professionals. These students' commitment to Miami communities predates the INUSE initiative. Dr. Jose Szapocznik,

Director of the Center for Family Studies, revisits their experiences in his essay, "Building Healthy Communities."

The Center for Ethics and Public Service, the outreach component of the University of Miami's School of Law, has established the CEDAD (Community Economic Development and Design Project) to provide small business counseling and training in economic development to residents of lowincome neighborhoods throughout Miami-Dade County. Over the last year the Center for Ethics and Public Services has also become actively engaged in initiatives with the Center for Urban and Community Design to help West Coconut Grove residents realize the potential of their community as a selfsustaining family-oriented neighborhood.

ABOUT THIS BOOK

As the descriptions above indicate, INUSE efforts in West Coconut Grove are still in an early phase. Although we have managed to launch a number of important pilot efforts, most of our work to date has attempted to assess the lay of the land: to literally map out the variety of people, places, issues and memories that combine to make up this neighborhood.

The somewhat mosaic nature of this study, therefore, reflects the groundup approach we have taken so far. We wanted each student and faculty member, each resident and community leader, to feel empowered to explore the elements of West Grove culture that means most to them.

By beginning to forge strong new relationships between the university and the community, and within the university itself, however, this experiment has revealed the effectiveness of reaching beyond single projects and unrelated social programs. What has emerged is a holistic perspective on how important it is to envision a neighborhood from many disciplines, to respect each of its unique characteristics, and observe and listen as much as we teach and tell.

Through this work we are seeing how a university, when it unleashes its resources, can yield lifelong learning for all of its participants, and carry out research that can be a catalyst for positive change.

FOOTNOTES

1.   Plans call for the architecture of the school to reflect the Bahamian heritage of the West Grove; for the school to include spaces to encourage families to participate in school activities; and for the school to host performances and other events that attempt to build bridges to the community at large through story-telling and artistic reflections on past and present events.

Photo courtesy of Arva Moore Parks

Photo: Nic DeGracia

History of West Coconut Grove

Arva Moore Parks

They knew the sea, these island people. Nurtured by tropical trade winds and crystal waters, for generations they had called Eleuthera, Harbour Island and New Providence their home. They understood island ways—reefs and shoals, calm and storm. The sea's bounty was theirs for the taking— tropical fish of a thousand colors, twisted shells cloistering hidden delicacies, flotsam from wrecks. They worked the difficult, rocky land, planting vegetables and tropical fruits in the coral-pocked flatlands and building simple, cool dwellings on the mangrove shores.

In time, other islands called them from across the wide gulf stream of new opportunity. They came to a foreign soil yet found familiar surroundings in places like Key West, Matacumbe, Key Vaca and Key Largo. Here, under Florida skies, they recreated their old way of life—turtling, wrecking, sponging, fishing and planting.

Although the settlements on the Keys flourished, the nearby Florida mainland was mostly uninhabited except for a small group of Seminoles who avoided capture and removal during the Seminole Wars. Except for the Indians, until the late 1870s, few people called this forgotten frontier home. Down Biscayne Bay from the Miami River, where the shoreline curved, an Englishman, Jack Peacock, had settled with his family. He joined two Bahamian families, the Pents and the Frows, who carved out homesteads nearby. Locals called this isolated settlement "Jack's Bight," although in 1874 a long-gone settler, Dr. Horace P. Porter, opened a long-forgotten post office there called Cocoanut Grove.

Jack Peacock convinced his brother Charles, Charles' wife Isabella and their three boys to come to the Bay Country. They found Jack's Bight so isolated and the surroundings so jungle-like that they retreated to old Fort Dallas on the Miami River. Here, they met a young visiting Staten Islander, Ralph M. Munroe. This fortuitous, history-making meeting brought the people together who would give birth to Coconut Grove, South Florida's most historic place.

In 1884, at Munroe's urging, Charles and Isabella opened a small inn called the Bay View House in Coconut Grove. Munroe brought his friends from the north, making the small hotel an instant success. To help with their growing clientele, Peacock went to Key West to seek workers. The first to come was Mariah Brown from Upper Bogue, Eleuthera. As the inn continued to grow, Mariah convinced several of her relatives and friends from Eleuthera and Harbour Island to join her in the Grove. From this nucleus of related Bahamian families, the West Grove began.

At first the workers lived on the grounds of the Bay View House. As their numbers increased, they moved just beyond the narrow footpath that ran behind the inn and the bayfront homes. Joseph Frow, a white Bahamian, sold them lots on the original street they called Evangelist Street, later Charles Avenue, after Frow's son. The settlement, named Kebo, after the African Mountain, shared not only physical proximity with the white community but also respect. The pioneers, both black and white, worshiped together in the Union Chapel and interacted for special occasions. Although the communities were separate, strict segregation laws did not come until the 1890s and until then, the two Grove communities were remarkably connected.

Paul Ransom hired many West Grove families to work at his Pine Knot Camp. Ransom was close to the Black community and often included them in camp activities.

Nat Sampson and Alice Burrows represented towo of the early Bahamian families who settled in what is now called West Grove.

As Ralph Munroe brought more of his northern friends into the area, the Kebo settlement grew. Bahamian workers provided the major workforce for the community as a whole and helped newcomers learn to live in the isolated, tropical land. They knew how to grow things in the unwelcoming terrain, how to plant tropical fruits in small rock craters, how to grub the pineland. They brought young saplings from the Bahamas and planted the seeds of their favorite fruits: sapodillas, caneps, almonds and tamarinds all over the Grove. They shared their knowledge of food, bush medicine and tropical gardening. Much of the lush landscaping in the Grove today was originally inspired by their memories of home.

Grovites, both black and white, saw themselves as different from the rest of Miami. Though law strictly enforced segregation, the kind of racism and Ku Klux Klan raids experienced by the residents of Overtown were very uncommon in the Grove. In fact, Overtown residents often fled to the Grove for safety. Many of the residents of "Colored Grove" and "White Grove," as the areas were known until the 60s, knew each other well. The two small communities sat in close proximity and many of the residents of today's West Grove worked in the homes of the white residents. As a result, many families developed warm feelings for each other.

From its beginning in 1891 and continuing for more than a century, the Housekeeper's Club, the pioneer women's club in white Coconut Grove, worked to improve the living conditions in West Grove. Sometimes members would solicit money from wealthy Northern win-

ter residents to buy schoolbooks and provide needed medical care. Often the Housekeepers Club members joined forces with organized groups in the black community to achieve common goals.

The denominational connection of several churches, particularly the Methodist and Episcopal, also brought the two communities together. These connections were more formally cemented in 1948 when Father Theodore Gibson, the priest at Christ Episcopal Church, spoke to the all-white Coconut Grove Civic Club about the deplorable conditions in Black Grove. Following the talk, Elizabeth Virrick, a petite white woman, asked Gibson how she could help. Together, the two leaders called a meeting at the American Legion Hall on McFarlane Road. From this unprecedented biracial gathering of more than 350 people, the Coconut Grove Citizens Committee for Slum Clearance came into being. This tenacious group, filled with the best citizens from both communities, succeeded in bringing in water mains and outlawing the privy. They maintained single-family and duplex zoning in much of West Grove, created parks and childcare facilities and generally upgraded the entire West Grove neighborhood.

The West Grove continued to grow but sometimes in a way the original families disliked. Many of the small single-family homes were torn down and what the residents called "concrete monsters" took their place. These apartments, mostly owned by absentee landlords, robbed the West Grove of some of its unique neighborhood feeling and brought in an unwelcome criminal element. Often the apartment dwellers did not share the proud heritage of the original Bahamian families and, as a

In the late 1880s, Black Bahamians came to Coconut Grove to work at the Bayview House, later called the Peacock Inn. At first they lived on Inn property until they built their own homes on Evangelist Street, now Charles Avenue.

New Yorker Paul Ransom discovered Coconut Grove in 1893. Three years later he opened Pine Knot Camp for boys that became the Florida Adirondack School in 1903. Today, it continues in the same location as Ransom Everglades School.

result, they felt like outsiders. In addition, many of the original families prospered and moved to the new suburban community of Richmond Heights, robbing the West Grove of some of its leadership. Despite these changes, strong unifying elements remained. George Washington Carver Elementary, Junior and Senior High Schools and the many churches were the linchpin and the continuing source of pride to those who called West Grove home.

In the 1960s, when the Civil Rights Movement swept America, it is not surprising that Father Gibson emerged as the leader of Miami's civil rights efforts. As president of the Miami branch of the NAACP from 1954 to 1965, Gibson was at the forefront of desegregating Miami's schools, beaches, golf courses and buses. He was even able to persuade some of his white Coconut Grove friends to join the NAACP and support the cause. He led the fight to remove the walls that divided, both figuratively and literally, the white and black communities. When school pairings came in 1971, he was the one that insisted that Carver Elementary and Junior High School remain open and that white children should be bused in to help achieve integration. This was in contrast to the situation that occurred two years earlier, when Carver Senior High had been closed and its former students sent to Coral Gables High School.

Although white students came into the West Grove to attend elementary and junior high school, the closing of Carver Senior High was a terrible loss to West Grove and the young men and women who no longer felt the nurturing and special attention their predecessors once received. Sadly, too, the Carver elementary and junior high no longer belonged exclusively to the West Grove. Integration came, but the children and the community of West Grove felt a sense of loss that at the time went unrecognized.

The early Bahamian families who founded and built West Grove left an indelible mark on Coconut Grove and all of South Florida. Many of their ancestors continue to live in the West Grove today and give South Florida a unique, almost singular connection with its past. Their achievements are widely recognized. Today, development pressures and an eroding core threaten the West Grove like never before as the children of middle class families move elsewhere. What a terrible thing it would be to lose this shrinking, historic community with its simple island-style homes, tropical ambiance and deep sense of pride. Sadder still would be the loss of the place that holds the memories of a proud and determined people who, despite great odds, left an unrivaled legacy.

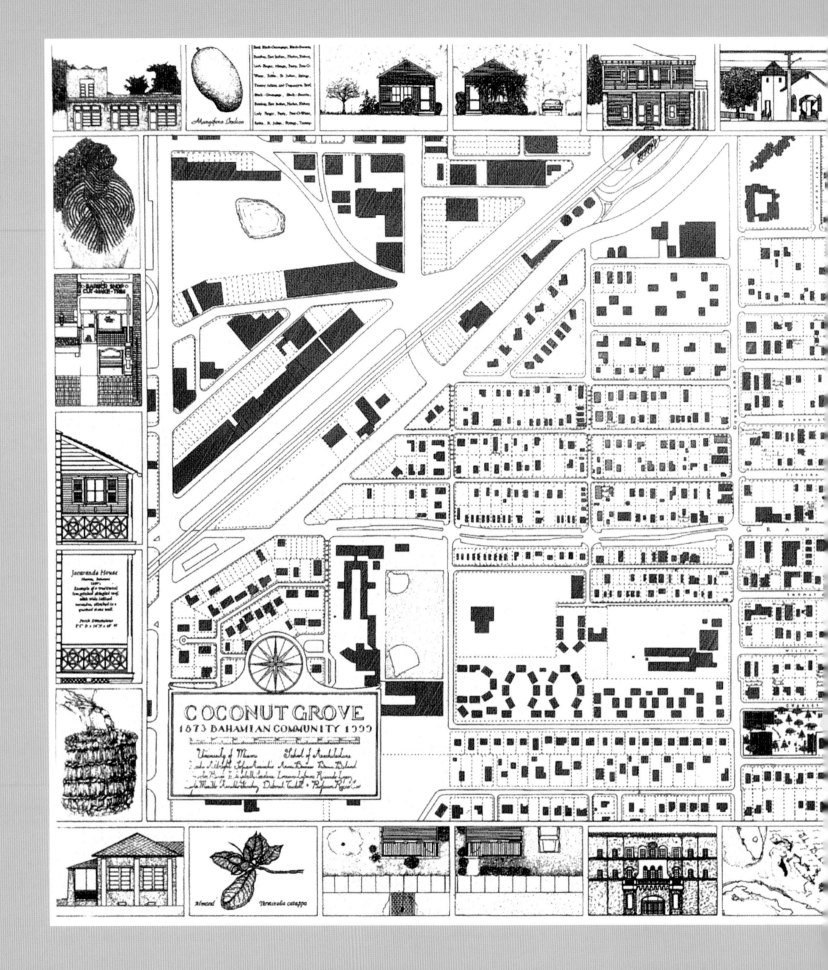

COCONUT GROVE
1873 BAHAMIAN COMMUNITY 1999

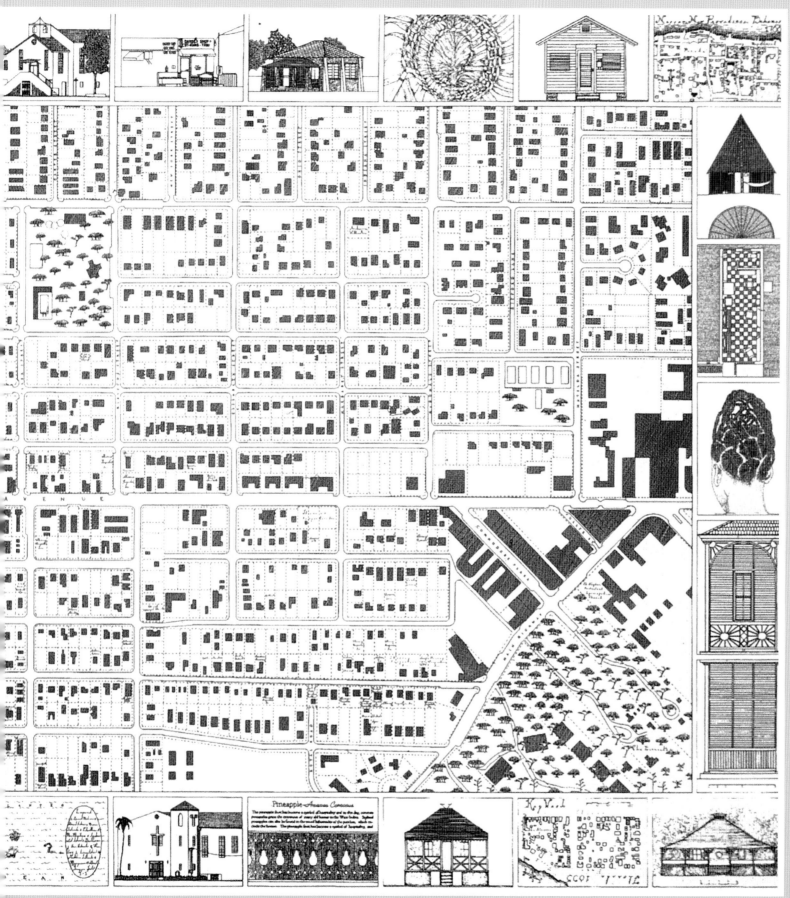

A map of West Coconut Grove, documenting the built, natural, historical and cultural artifacts of the place and region as well as its plan and ownership patterns. The map was produced by students in architecture studio focusing on the design of a new school for the community, taught by Professor Rocco Ceo.

Oral Histories
West Grove Thematic Quotes

Gregory W. Bush
University of Miami School of Arts & Sciences
Department of History

Photo: Miranda Mulligan

REMEMBERING EARLIER DAYS

In Coconut Grove, we had Colored Town and White Town. That happened because a lot of Bahamians came here. I lived in the section called Colored Town. We lived on Charles Avenue. All my childhood was on Charles Avenue in Coconut Grove. All through my childhood it was Colored Town. Coconut Grove was just a little village town with dirt roads and no street lights and no running water when I came along. I went away to school in 1944, at which time they really had very few apartment buildings. And when I came back, there were these apartments. I could call everybody by name as a child going to school. And when I came back, here were all these strange people in my town. That was the first time I really realized what is meant by saying, "You can't go home again," because if you leave and you come back just a year or two later and it's a different town. And so then, they started calling it West Grove by the time I got back in '47- '48. I still call it our section of Coconut Grove.

You have to remember that in those days we didn't have television. So, the only things you

Photo: Miranda Mulligan

could do was to go to church, to school and on Saturdays to a movie. We could go to the Ace Theater. We'd go to the movies on Saturday, and we could go to the Dew Drop Inn, which was the Dunn's drugstore. On Sunday afternoons, you went to church in the morning. You went to Sunday School at three o'clock, and you went to Young People's Service League at six. The only place you could go in between was to the Dew Drop Inn. The few times you got to go out to dinner, we'd go to the Wallace's Restaurant there.
Thelma Anderson Gibson

SOCIAL LIFE

Funerals have always been a time of community gathering, where the community gathers to share a common loss, but also to provide comfort, and hope, and encouragement to a bereaved family. You will find that even today, a funeral is an occasion that you simply attend. It's not like what happens out east, I saw this so many times. I had funerals, even in my parish, where sometimes the church would be half-empty. People just didn't see this as part of the community, which included them. It's your loss so you deal with it the best way you can. That is not so with the black community in the Grove. Many times, it's a very private kind of affair, but it's something which draws out the entire community.

Reverend Austin Cooper

When you attend 6th grade, you have a high school education. My father had finished that and he was the top person in his class. He said it was time for him to come to America to see if he could get a job over there to take care of his family. One thing about my father, he sent my parents, my grandparents, something every week. He had another brother and another sister. My father was the caretaker of everybody.

Them who came over with my father gave him their money to keep. That's the type of individual my father was. They didn't have to worry about no body taking that money because all of them respected him and knew that whatever was missing he would replace it. That's why they called him "father." Even the grown men, always called him father.

Vernika Silva

We had what you call the Sunday school and then we had the young people's service week practiced by the youth. That's where we learned about the types of services and the type of individuals that conduct the services. What we call the blessed days and the days that we should know about like All Saints Days, and Thanksgiving service.

Vernika Silva

One of the things about that is that they, those children, lived in Coconut Grove and my grandparents married. They all basically grew up in this community also and were a part of the daily life and everybody basically knew each other. My grandmother, and my great grandmother, the house she built was like the only home on the street that had electricity at that time and it was like an open house because not only her children, but other families in the community, children in the community, were also like a part of the house. Everybody knew everybody really and it was a small community and there were certain families that you knew you always had a place to come and get a meal or a place to stay over night in.

Yvonne McDonald

Photo: Morgan McGinn

In the late 40's, early 50's, you have people like Father Gibson who was involved very heavily in trying to do something about the conditions and that is when we started looking at how we can improve the community.

When we talk about this community, people talk church and how that was the social life.
Yvonne McDonald

Loretta: The circus was also really popular. They would come every January.
Blanche: The circus had a sign up to make us look, read, and run...because my daddy took us and we were large enough to read, and we showed him the sign, and then he had to bring us back.
Loretta: You couldn't go up there in a white shirt. They'd say, "What you doin' wearin' a white shirt, nigger? Take it off!" I tell you...we had a hard time. But you know...we gonna get it straight!
Leona Cooper-Baker Group Interview

Knowledge Building as Community Building: Universities and Civic Engagement

Robin Bachin
Charlton w. Tebeau Associate Professor
University o fMiami School of Arts & Sciences
Department of History

In her 2003 keynote address at the Imagining America conference, University of Illinois Chancellor Nancy Cantor (now president of Syracuse University) championed the role of universities as a public good. "We educate the next generation of leaders," she explained. "We address important societal issues with discoveries that change our world. We preserve our cultural past while laying the groundwork for the future. And we experiment with ways of building community."[1] This last idea, that universities have a critical role to play in building community, addressed one of the founding principals of the Imagining American consortium, a group of colleges and universities dedicated to promoting the civic mission of higher education. They call for an ethic of collaboration between universities and their communities whereby scholars, students, activists, and residents can join together in the act of knowledge building.[2] This process recognizes that different groups bring different kinds of expertise, and all have a vital role to play in fostering connections between people and across cultures. By engaging more directly with community, universities not only bring skills and resources to the public but also transform the process of knowledge production itself by fostering a symbiotic relationship with people and groups outside of the confines of the campus. This act of "collaborative co-creation," as historian David Scobey calls it, places knowledge-building and culture-making at the heart of democratic public life, thereby reconnecting the university with its publics.[3]

This emphasis on civic engagement as one of the primary goals of higher education has resulted from the increasing distance between academia and the public in the last century. As universities pursued specialized research at the expense of broad humanitarian engagement, they contributed to the increased segmentation between academic work and the promotion of civic activities outside university walls. This culture of expertise also brought with it specialization and differentiation among academic disciplines, leading to greater fragmentation within the university curriculum. Examining the shifting contours of the relationship between the academy and community in the last century can help us understand methods by which they may be reconnected, and in the process help reinvigorate the public sphere at the start of the twenty-first century.[4]

Philosopher and educator John Dewey laid the foundation for promoting civic engagement through education at the turn of the last century. Dewey believed in the intimate connections between the search for knowledge, the process of social engagement, and democracy. He wrote, "Democracy is freedom. If truth is at the bottom of things, freedom means giving truth a chance to show itself, a chance to well up from the depths."[5] For Dewey, truth was not a static entity, but rather something that emerged through the process of human experience and social interaction within communities. Dewey played a leading role in articulating the place of emerging research universities at the turn of the century. According to Dewey, knowledge and truth were not contained within the walls of the university. Instead, he believed in the social foundation of knowledge. The processes of shaping knowledge and building community would be dynamic and dialogic; they would inform one another and unravel in new and spontaneous ways. The academy and the public, then, together would be engaged in the creation of democracy and the revitalization of the public sphere.[6]

This idea of shaping knowledge through experience with community conditions was especially important for urban universities. Dewey and other progressive educators believed that the university had a unique and significant role to play in addressing social issues faced by surrounding communities. For Dewey, this connection formed the basis of an informed and engaged citizenry. In Democracy and Education, he wrote that "a democracy is more than a form of government; it is primarily a mode of associated living, of conjoint communicated experience."[7] In other words, the best way for universities to foster democracy was through engaged, experiential learning. That meant working with faculty members from disciplines such as the emerging fields of sociology, psychology, and social work, as well as with local community groups such as religious leaders, union organizers, and

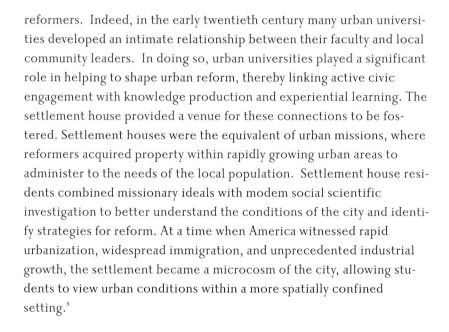

Living Traditions of Coconut Grove exhibit, Lowe Art Museum, University of Miami

reformers. Indeed, in the early twentieth century many urban universities developed an intimate relationship between their faculty and local community leaders. In doing so, urban universities played a significant role in helping to shape urban reform, thereby linking active civic engagement with knowledge production and experiential learning. The settlement house provided a venue for these connections to be fostered. Settlement houses were the equivalent of urban missions, where reformers acquired property within rapidly growing urban areas to administer to the needs of the local population. Settlement house residents combined missionary ideals with modern social scientific investigation to better understand the conditions of the city and identify strategies for reform. At a time when America witnessed rapid urbanization, widespread immigration, and unprecedented industrial growth, the settlement became a microcosm of the city, allowing students to view urban conditions within a more spatially confined setting.[8]

Settlement residents recognized the role of the settlement in providing a training ground for university students in the social sciences, but saw the settlement as much more than a laboratory. Jane Addams, co-founder in 1889 of Hull House in Chicago, voiced this perspective when she explained, "I have always objected to the phrase 'sociological laboratory' applied to us, because Settlements should be something much more human and spontaneous than such a phrase connotes."[9] Indeed, for Addams, the settlement represented an arena in which active participation in civic life, along with social scientific investigation, could foster a new vision of social democracy that emerged from the ground up, just as Dewey envisioned.

Efforts of settlement house residents in cities across the country focused on sociological surveys of the city, aesthetic improvement, and social reform, and saw these processes as interconnected. Settlements worked alongside municipal art societies and neighborhood improvement associations to fight for beautification projects such as street lighting, billboard reform, civic sculpture, and public parks. They joined these beautification efforts with larger-scale urban reform projects, including tenement house reform, smoke abatement, sanitation, and factory inspection laws. These grass-roots efforts in cities such as New York, Baltimore, Chicago, Hartford, and Philadelphia highlighted the linkages between the improvement of physical space and the promotion of social connectedness.

These localized efforts at urban improvement formed the foundation of the City Beautiful movement in the early twentieth century. The City Beautiful movement represented one of the first efforts in America to create comprehensive plans for urban growth. It reflected the ideas of a new generation of city boosters who looked both to aesthetic enhancement and to scientific models of problem solving in their quest to control and shape urban growth. Numerous city plans, including the 1902 McMillan Plan for Washington, D.C. and Daniel Burnham's Plans for San Francisco (1905) and Chicago (1909), embodied this new idea of planning, and highlighted the relationships among commercial growth, efficiency, and beauty in shaping cities for the future. These plans illustrated the links between consolidated planning and urban design, which combined an aesthetic sensibility with practical functionalism.[10]

For a brief moment, the goals and strategies of educators, social reformers, and the emerging field of planning came together. In 1909, three settlement house workers—Mary Simkovitch, Florence Kelley, and Lillian Wald—organized the first annual National Conference on City Planning. It brought together reformers, architects, landscape architects, political leaders, and commercial and real estate groups to address methods of improving America's cities. According to Simkovitch, the goal was to "use planning to deal with social problems." The organizers of the conference explained that "city planning for social and economic ends will logically result in a genuinely and completely beautiful city." This conference highlighted how Dewey's ideas about the importance of linking the quest for knowledge with broad-based public participation could forge a new model of community engagement and social democracy.[11]

These connections very quickly broke down, however, as the field of planning (much like other emerging disciplines) became more highly professionalized and lost much of its emphasis on community engagement and social reform. Increasingly planners emphasized not only the importance of efficient design and land use, but also the need for expertly supervised urban landscapes that would ensure the best models of civic stewardship. Planner Benjamin Marsh captured this emerging idea of planning as a specialized process when he claimed in 1909, "City planning is the adaptation of a city to its proper function."[12] This desire to impose disciplinary order on cities represented what planning historian Christine Boyer has called the "planning mentality," and signaled a departure from the more localized, grass-roots efforts at reform that characterized the efforts of an earlier generation. Instead of city planning being part of a broader social reform agenda, with local civic activists and business leaders appointed to planning commissions, the field increasingly was dominated by professional planners trained in university programs who saw little connection between their plans and the reformists agenda of local activists.[13]

This emphasis on expertly controlled, comprehensive urban planning mirrored developments within the academy by the 1920s. The process of professionalization within the social sciences led to greater distance between academics and the communities they investigated. University-trained sociologists increasingly studied the city as detached observers, claiming the importance of neutrality and objectivity in gathering and interpreting data. Scholars emphasized their role as experts in using positivist approaches to identifying urban "pathologies," rather than engaging with a variety of urban residents to foster dynamic civic engagement. The Chicago School of Sociology played a leading role in formulating this positivist approach to studying the city. As University of Chicago sociologist Ernest W. Burgess explained, "If neighborhood work can have a scientific basis, it is because there are social forces in community life--forces like geographical conditions, human wishes, community consciousness--that can be studied, described, analyzed, and ultimately measured."[14] The language he uses to describe "neighborhood work" is that of the scientific investigator who can quantify data and objectively present findings. The more messy and spontaneous process of shaping knowledge and fostering social reform through broad-based coalition-building loses out to the guidance of scientific experts. Like the move toward comprehensive planning, then, the culture of expertise within academia brought with it a process of retrenchment from the public realm.[15]

The specialization among academics also shaped new models of urban planning. By the 1930s and 1940s, planning became a tool of an increasingly interventionist state, both at the municipal and federal levels. Governments turned to planning professionals to reshape cities and promote economic recovery through a new focus on practical problems facing the city, including housing and economic revitalization. University-trained experts, including engineers, public policy analysts, and social scientists, comprised municipally -controlled planning commissions that identified and gave form to "the public interest." As planning became more professionalized and technocratic, there was less and less room either for aesthetic considerations or for widespread public participation.

The quintessential model of this kind of government planning official was Robert Moses, who took the position as New York City Park Commissioner in 1934. Moses was given vast reign not only over park development, but also over the creation and destruction of urban infrastructure. He approached urban planning as a policy expert, identifying problems, creating solutions, and instituting them at will. This positivist planning model became the basis for one of the most dramatic transformations of the urban landscape in America, slum clearance and high-rise public housing. The increasing role of the federal government in urban planning issues only tightened this connection between planning, public policy expertise, and government-led design. The 1949 Housing Act, which made slum clearance, the construction of public housing, and the creation of municipal and regional plans central goals of the federal government, further enshrined the model of expert planners and policy advisors imposing their plans on neighborhoods with little consideration for public input.[16]

Indeed, the Pruit-t-Igoe public housing project in St. Louis, built in 1956 and partially razed in 1972, became the embodiment of all that was wrong with this planning model--little consideration of design in shaping public housing, and no input from residents whose lives and homes were affected by planning decisions. New York Times architecture critic Herbert Muschamp has gone so far as to speak of "the violence imposed on the cityscape by modern planning and urban renewal concepts."[17] The ideas that formed the early foundation of the City Beautiful movement, and of urban reform more broadly—aesthetic enhancement, community cohesion, and engagement with a wide range of community participants—broke down during the period of the Great Depression and World War II. Planners began to function as tools of the state, with a direct connection forged between university-trained experts and government bureaucracies. Knowledge and expertise emanated from the top down, unlike in Dewey's formulation in which truth would "well up from the depths."[18]

It was against this bureaucratic mentality that Jane Jacobs reacted in her classic 1961 study, The Death and Life of Great American Cities. For Jacobs and other critics of urban renewal, the meaning of city life was defined by "the web of casual public life." "City planning," she argued, "neither respects spontaneous self-diversification among city populations nor contrives to provide for it."[19] What was needed in cities, she claimed, was less planning and more spontaneity. Grass-roots movements in the 1960s and 1970s gave voice to the concerns of many urban residents whose interests had been silenced for decades. The successes of the Civil Rights movement and the rise of the environmental and women's movements highlighted the willingness of American citizens to confront conditions facing their communities and challenge government to reshape policy.

These calls for increased public participation in decision-making

processes came at the same time that academics across the nation challenged the entrenched bureaucracies of universities and the balkanization of knowledge production. Radical scholars in the 1960s and 1970s critiqued specialization within their disciplines, and called for community activism as the basis for new models of learning and civic connection. Scholars in a variety of humanities and social science fields argued that research had become too narrow, technical, and detached. According to Julie Reuben, a historian of education, "Under the guise of objectivity, universities and disciplines came to favor a certain style of research, dispassionate and aloof."[20] Scholars called for a host of changes, including more open admissions policies, less stringent disciplinary boundaries, and reward for scholars who engaged directly with communities outside of the university walls.

Planners and planning educators echoed these critiques. The most vocal critic of the state of the planning profession in the 1960s was Paul Davidoff, professor of city planning at Hunter College and the University of Pennsylvania. He argued that the practice of planning had become myopic, limiting itself to physical planning rather than city planning. Physical planning focused on the comprehensive arrangement of land and buildings, but paid little attention to the broader issues facing cities. "A city is its people, their practices, and their political, social, cultural and economic institutions as well as other things," he argued.[21] He pointed to the failure of urban renewal and public housing to illustrate the high costs of having the planner act solely as a technician. Instead, he called for "plural planning," in which the planner acts as an advocate for the needs of neighborhoods. The basis of this advocacy planning was Davidoff's belief in "the need to establish an effective urban democracy, one in which citizens may be able to play an active role in the process of deciding public policy."[22] He called for planning schools to reevaluate their curricula in order to broaden the scope of planning. Planners must be trained to deal with the physical shape of the city, but more importantly, to coordinate the myriad of functions which comprise urban communities. Only through a substantive understanding of social work, law, history, and civic design could the next generation of planners effectively and thoughtfully prescribe the future of urban life.

Many of the ideas articulated by Davidoff were put into practice at Pratt

Institute in Brooklyn, New York. In 1963, planning department director George Raymond created the Pratt Institute Center for Community and Environmental Development (PICCED). The Center institutionalized the ideas of advocacy planning, and served as a model for other institutions across the nation. The Center focused on community-based development, working with local community organizations to identify goals, devise strategies for change, and implement plans. Pratt offered not only architectural services but also comprehensive design and financing plans for projects organized by neighborhood associations. Some of PICCED's projects have included the creation of the Pratt Architecture Collaborative to provide designs and working blueprints for groups involved in construction of low-cost housing; the formation of the New York City Housing and Community Development Coalition to act as a unified lobbying force for neighborhood groups; the construction and rehabilitation of thousands of units of low-income housing; and the development of a five-week training program in community organizing, real estate financing, and program development. All of PICCED's programs highlight the important role planners can play not just in physical planning but also in community action.[23]

The education students receive in this type of program differs from that of traditional planning programs. According to current director Ron Shiffman, "Our students are not the traditional students. We have as our students the neighborhood in which we work. We have as our students ourselves and our volunteers who work with us, as well as regular students. The interaction among all of us in learning about our urban environment. . . creates a unique educational experience."[24] This belief in the symbiotic process of learning, through which students and teachers learn from one another as well as from neighborhood residents and community leaders, reflects Dewey's vision of truth and knowledge emerging directly from experience in the community. And Shiffman shares both Dewey and Jane Addam's understanding of the relationships among knowledge, community engagement, and democracy. "We do not look at the community as a laboratory. We see [PICCED] as a service that is very much part of the social change movement."[25]

While advocacy planning reflected many of the ideas about social justice and shared authority that characterized social movements of the 1960s and 1970s, the ability of planners to sustain these goals proved more difficult in the 1980s. Many planning scholars have pointed to the difficulties faced by advocacy planning, and planning in general, when federal funds for planning and other urban initiatives dried up in the 1980s. While programs like PICCED survived, most planners and planning departments instead focused on courting the private sector to facilitate the development process. As private development replaced government initiatives in everything from housing to community design, planners often found themselves working as consultants to specific clients rather than as mediators among a variety of different constituents.[26]

In addition, the university came to be viewed as a source of expertise, transferring technology and information to the private sector and guiding government agencies in economic development. With universities also becoming more reliant on private donors and large research grants in the face of shrinking government support, the future of the engaged university was in question. Indeed, by the 1990s many scholars and university administrators called into question the mission of higher education. The 1999 American Association of Colleges and Universities Presidents' Fourth of July Declaration on the Civic Responsibility of Higher Education challenged educators "to reexamine its public purposes and its commitment to the democratic ideal." It called on universities to become more engaged, through actions and teaching, with its communities, both local and national. What was at stake, according to these educators, was the very future of American democracy.[27]

This process of rethinking the direction of higher education had profound implications not only for the structure of the curriculum and the recruitment of students, but also for the relationship between universities and their communities. Many institutions looked to civic engagement with local communities as the way to revive the broader humanitarian goals of higher education articulated a century ago by Dewey. Combining community involvement with cross-disciplinary learning, these programs have highlighted how the production and transmission of knowledge are not linear, top-down processes, but rather spontaneous and surprising endeavors in which all involved—student, teacher, community resident—have something to contribute and something to learn.[28]

The University of Pennsylvania formed one of the most comprehensive

Professor Robin Bachin lecturing on the West Grove.

programs in town-gown relations and service learning when it launched its Center for Community Partnerships in 1992. The Center is based on three core ideas: that the futures of the University and the surrounding community of West Philadelphia are intertwined; that Penn can make a significant contribution to improving the quality of life in West Philly; and Penn can enhance its overall mission of advancing and transmitting knowledge by helping to improve the quality of life in West Philly. The Center aims to create new partnerships linking the University with the community, and has done so in a variety of ways. It has created University-assisted community schools that function as centers of education, services, and activities for students, their parents, and other community members. The Center also initiated the Volunteers in Public Service program to coordinate the volunteer efforts of Penn faculty, students and alumni. The Community Arts Partnership advances academically-based community service by Penn faculty and students in collaboration with West Philadelphia community-based artists and organizations to create or expand arts programs in local public schools. The Community Outreach Partnership Center works with leaders in West Philadelphia to address issues including minority entrepreneurship, infrastructure concerns, education and job training, and non-profit community organization development. The Center coordinates a number of other outreach programs that build upon the idea that university-community collaboration enhances the overall mission of higher education.[29]

The Great Cities Initiative (GCI) at the University of Illinois at Chicago (UIC) is another example of an urban institution whose mission is one of civic engagement. By creating, disseminating and applying interdisciplinary knowledge in Community Development, Metropolitan Sustainability, Workforce Development, and Professional Education, the Institute works to improve the quality of life in metropolitan Chicago and other national and international urban areas. GCI brings UIC's metropolitan commitment to first class research in and for the "great cities" of the world -- with a particular emphasis on Chicago. The UIC Neighborhood Initiative, part of the GCI, provides a university-community partnership with neighborhoods adjacent to the UIC campus. Ironically, the initial construction and later expansion of UIC in the 1970s and 1980s was responsible for part of Jane Addams' Hull House being razed. Through the Neighborhood Initiative the University now works with leaders of Hull House to preserve Addams'

goals of making the West Side of Chicago a site of engaged learning and social improvement. In addition, UIC's City Design Center gives planning and architecture students a chance to make linkages among theory, practice, and social interests through their work with West Side community groups. Part of the mission of the City Design Center is to promote a dialogue about the relationship between the designed urban environment and the diversity of the city's cultural, economic, and political life, the goals advocated by Paul Davidoff decades earlier. Past projects of the City Design Center include collaborative design of a local playground; designing a cooperative marketplace; creating a commercial feasibility study for the Near West Side; and developing programs to move public housing residents to home ownership.[30]

The University of Michigan has created a number of programs that link education with community service, and that rethink the undergraduate curriculum to promote interdisciplinary learning through project-based initiatives. The University's Detroit Community Outreach Partnership Center (DCOPC) is based on a community-planning model in which the processes of learning and planning are collaborative in nature. This emphasis on collaboration has led participants to attempt to move beyond the provision of technical assistance, where one side provides expertise to the other. Instead, student teams from fields including law, architecture, urban planning, landscape architecture, natural resources planning, public policy and business work with community groups in on-going projects that have real-world results for neighborhoods. For example, students and faculty in an urban planning course did inventory work, case study background investigation, and a preliminary site plan for a housing development in a Detroit Empowerment Zone. A graduate architecture studio followed up with designs for energy-efficient housing. Law students worked with community groups and developers to negotiate and draft agreements for housing construction while urban planning students conducted a feasibility study for new commercial development to complement the new housing.[31]

The Arts of Citizenship Program at the University of Michigan takes the DCOPC one step further. It uses design and other community-based projects to link learning with community service, but does so by inserting the humanities into the mix. The Arts of Citizenship Program is an effort to build new bridges between the university and the larger community in the arts and humanities. "Just as a bridge goes two ways," explains its mission statement, "the Program has a double mission. We believe that the work of scholars and artists can do much to enrich civic and community life in America. And we believe that pursuing such work in public, and in dialogue with the public, can do much to enrich university research, teaching, and creative expression."[32] Director David Scobey calls the Program "both a civic and an intellectual experiment."[33] Projects include neighborhood design initiatives in Detroit, public history projects with regional museums and educational institutions, and collaborations with national cultural agencies and community partnership programs throughout the country. The Students on Site teaching partnership brings together University students and faculty, and Ann Arbor teachers and students, to use local neighborhoods as sites for community-based, interdisciplinary teaching. The program has helped develop writing and art projects in local schools, encouraged students to think ecologically about their neighborhoods through field trips to teach them about the environmental history of the Huron River watershed, and created a Web site to serve as an online teaching archive of documents about the history of the Ann Arbor. The Web site includes over 250 documents-including maps, photographs, audio recordings, newspaper articles, and personal letters to serve as a resource to local students and teachers.[34]

These initiatives are about more than community outreach. They fundamentally change the way we think about the role of higher education and its relationship to communities beyond the walls of the university. There are new pedagogical models that emerge from these partnerships. Faculty and students learn from reflection about action and experience, not just from books and lectures. These collaborations force educators to rethink the sites of knowledge production. New means of learning and understanding emerge when a site outside of the university becomes the locus of exploration. According to David Scobey, when the Arts of Citizenship Program began working with local neighborhood groups, a "new set of possibilities opened up: the possibility of a university-based initiative that integrated national cultural debates with local projects, civic collaboration with intellectual experiments, place with profession."[35]

Numerous institutions across the country have developed similar models of civic engagement. The Center for Democracy and Citizenship at the University of Minnesota aims to "develop community based civic

projects so that young people can learn civic skills, and people have opportunities to practice civic engagement."[36] The Sustainable Cities Program at the University of Southern California allows students to "transcend disciplinary boundaries and acquire a profound understanding of how collaborative, interdisciplinary, policy-relevant research on major environmental problems should be conducted."[37] These programs and others like them have worked hard to overcome institutional obstacles to interdisciplinary teaching and collaborative learning, obstacles that are firmly entrenched in many colleges and universities nationwide. In helping to break down these boundaries—between academic disciplines with the university, and between the university and the public—these efforts have helped forge a new model of the engaged university, one that will help restore the element of "education for citizenship" that is at the core of higher education.

It is this kind of civic connection that the University of Miami's Initiative for Urban and Social Ecology (INUSE) has brought to the greater Miami community. INUSE provides a refreshing model of town-gown collaboration that can reconnect elements of design and urban beautification with social welfare concerns within the larger public realm. By resituating knowledge production beyond the confines of the university, the program fosters a renewed understanding of Dewey's conception of the links between knowledge and democracy. At the same time, it helps break down the boundaries between disciplines that fragment the university curriculum and inhibit critical inquiry.

PLACE-MAKING, HISTORY, AND COMMUNITY IDENTITY

INUSE's efforts in West Coconut Grove have illustrated how the process of joining academic training with civic engagement, and urban design with social activism, can play central roles in establishing a strong sense of place and community identity. What goes into creating a sense of place? Natural landscapes that give places their character; the built environment that reflects the human imprint on the land; the civic institutions that help shape community; the human populations whose cultural traditions shape the character of place. But perhaps most important is the interaction between people and place over time. The sense of historical connection to a place, and the meanings and memories this connection conveys for people from different generations, fosters both a personal attachment and a feeling of shared communal commitment to that place. Recognizing the complex and multilayered history of a place plays a central role in creating a vision for its future, thereby weaving memories of the past into dreams for the future.

Some of the projects in this collection point to University-community collaborations designed to enhance this connection to the past. Oral histories, photographs, and historic preservation efforts jog memories and allow residents to feel a deeper sense of connection to the neighborhood. Recognizing the long history of inter-racial cooperation and community-based activism also can point today's University and community partners to strategies that united residents and influenced policy decisions in the past. As Arva Parks explains in her historical essay, the history of Coconut Grove inextricably links together blacks and whites, migrants from the Bahamas and travelers from up north. The Grove has a long history of inter-racial cooperation to promote urban improvement, and connecting this history to new planning, design, and arts projects can enhance the University/community collaborative process. After World War II, for example, black residents in Coconut Grove worked together with local businesspeople and civic leaders, both black and white, to address the increasingly poor housing conditions they faced. An article in the Ladies' Home Journal by reporter, activist, and pioneering environmentalist Marjory Stoneman Douglas entitled "Communities Face Their Slums," detailed the problematic conditions facing "Colored Town." Douglas described the overcrowding, dilapidated housing, lack of proper sanitation, use of unsafe well water, inadequate health care, and erratic garbage collection that plagued the area. She also recounted how, in the summer of 1948, Reverend Theodore R. Gibson, minister of Christ Episcopal Church, described conditions in the black Grove, stating, "My people are living Seven Deep." Gibson's speech led to the creation of the Coconut Grove Citizens Committee for Slum Clearance. Comprised of black and whites civic, religious, and business leaders, the Committee conducted extensive house-by-house surveys, investigating water and septic service, housing conditions, and income levels of residents. Committee members then petitioned city commissioners to conduct follow-up investigations and pass legislation to pass ordinances that would improve living conditions for residents. In describing the successes of the Citizens Committee, Douglass pointed out that it had awakened "the true value of citizenship and the importance of [blacks and whites] working together" in a spirit of "true neighborliness."[38]

Still, the Grove suffered many of the same setbacks in cooperative planning that other cities faced. By the 1960s, when the federally funded Neighborhood Development Program undertook a revitalization program in the black Grove, many residents felt left out of the planning process. Black Grovites, like their counterparts throughout the country, often equated urban renewal with "Negro removal." In response, several residents of the West Grove established BLACK GROVE. INC. in 1970 to take control of local planning efforts. According to Julie Allen Field, one of the founders, the goal of the organization was to take advantage of the most important resource of the community—it's people. "A sense of a close-knit community, a feeling of deep roots, of belonging to this place," explained Field, was the source of hope for the neighborhood's future.[39] BLACK GROVE, INC. represented a "coalition of knowledge" for the community," and brought together national planning practitioners with local activists. A poem by Warren Brodey called Black Grove Spirit captured this vision of the place and its people:

Black Grove is a CONSPIRACY
of living space.
It is a breathing in of life itself
Instead of being stifled
With products or science or services
Seeking to show people
That experts know best. . .
Black Grove is real grove of intensely real
life that
Knows it is not like the words
That are used to describe it or anything else.
It is a grove of black
And white people
Who know that each has a different heritage
To use in finding a way back
To the soundness of ecology
Before industrial destruction.[40]

The ideas so poignantly put forward in this poem still resonate today. Through collaboration with community groups, university faculty and students must learn the lessons of the past and understand their role as one of participating in a "coalition of knowledge" rather than one where they showcase their "expertise." Recognizing the variety of ideas, skills, and traditions that different groups bring to this process allows for a cooperative model of planning and community enrichment. And engaging with the community in multilayered ways, through history, the arts, planning, and design allows scholars, students, and community groups the chance to break down barriers between disciplines and among each other. This process of community building through knowledge building sets the stage for the university to truly become, in Nancy Cantor's words, a "public good."

FOOTNOTES

1.   Nancy Cantor, "Transforming America: The University as Public Good," *Foreseeable Futures #3* (Ann Arbor, MI: Imagining America, 2003), 4.

2.   See the mission statement for Imagining America: Artists and Scholars in Public Life on their Web site at ImaginingAmerica@umich.edu. The organization began in 1999 as a two-year program of the White House Millennium Council, and in 2001 became a national consortium of colleges and universities. Imagining America is based at the University of Michigan in the Office of the Vice President for Research.

3.   David Scobey, quoted from the roundtable discussion, "Research/Actions Action/Research: Strategies for Community/University Collaboration in the Arts and Humanities," American Studies Association Annual Meeting, Nov. 12, 2004.

4.   For further discussion of the shifting relationship between universities and their publics, and efforts to remedy this change, see the essays in Thomas Ehrlich, ed., *Civic Responsibility and Higher Education* (Phoenix, AZ: American Council on Education and Oryx Press, 2000).

5.   John Dewey, "Christianity and Democracy: An Address to the University of Michigan Christian Association" (March 27, 1892), in John Dewey, *The Early Works, 1882-1898*, Jo Ann Boydston et al., 5 vols. (Carbondale: Southern Illinois University Press, 1967-1972), 4.

6.   John Dewey, *Experience and Education* (New York: Collier Books, 1938), 82-86. For more on John Dewey's philosophy of education, see Robin F. Bachin, *Building the South Side: Urban Space and Civic Culture in Chicago, 1890-1919* (Chicago: University of Chicago Press, 2004), 67-72; Andrew Feffer, *The Chicago Pragmatists and American Progressivism* (Ithaca: Cornell University Press, 1993),117-123; Alan Ryan, *John Dewey and the High Tide of American Liberalism* (New York: W.W. Norton & Company, 1995) and Robert Westbrook, *John Dewey and American Democracy* (Ithaca: Cornell University Press, 1991).

7.   John Dewey, *Democracy and Education* (New York: Macmillan, 1916), 99.

8.   For further discussion of the history of settlement houses, see Mina Carson, *Settlement Folk: Social Thought and the Settlement Movement* (Chicago: University of Chicago Press, 1990); Allen F. Davis, *Spearheads for Reform: The Social Settlements and the Progressive Movement, 1890-1914* (New York: Oxford University Press, 1967); Elizabeth Lasch-Quinn,

Black Neighbors: Race and the Limits of Reform in the American Settlement House Movement, 1890-1945 (Chapel Hill: University of North Carolina Press, 1993); and Rivka Shpak Lissak, *Pluralism and Progressives: Hull House and the New Immigrants, 1890-1919* (Chicago: University of Chicago Press, 1989);

9.   Jane Addams, *Twenty Years at Hull-House* (1910; New York: Signet Books, 1960), 217.

10.   For further discussion of the City Beautiful movement, see William H. Wilson, *The City Beautiful Movement* (Baltimore: Johns Hopkins University Press, 1989).

11.   Quoted in Richard Fogelsong, *Planning the Capitalist City: The Colonial Era to the 1920s* (Princeton, NJ: Princeton University Press, 1986), 202-3.   For further discussion of female reformers' roles in shaping early planning ideas, see Susan Marie Wirka, "The City Social Movement: Progressive Women Reformers and Early Social Planning," in Mary Corbin Sies and Christopher Silver, eds., *Planning the Twentieth-Century American City* (Baltimore: Johns Hopkins University Press, 1996), 55-75. See also the *Proceedings of the First National Conference on City Planning, 1909*, Republished as *Senate Document 422, 61st Congress Second Session* (Washington, D.C.: Government Printing Office, 1910).

12.   Benjamin Clarke Marsh, *An Introduction to City Planning* (1909; New York: Arno Press, 1974), 27.

13.   M. Christine Boyer, *Dreaming the Rational City: The Myth of American City Planning* (Cambridge, MA: M.I.T. Press, 1983), 59-82.

14.   Ernest W. Burgess, "Can Neighborhood Work Have a Scientific Basis?" in Robert E. Park, Ernest W. Burgess, and Roderick D. McKenzie, eds. *The City* (Chicago: University of Chicago Press, 1925, 1967), 143.

15.   For further discussion of the Chicago School of Sociology, see Robert E.L. Faris, *Chicago Sociology, 1920-1932* (Chicago: University of Chicago Press, 1967); Lester R. Kurtz, *Evaluating Chicago Sociology: A Guide to the Literature, with an Annotated Bibliography* (Chicago: University of Chicago Press, 1984); and Stow Persons, *Ethnic Studies at Chicago, 1905-45* (Urbana: University of Illinois Press, 1987),

16.   See, for example, Boyer, *Dreaming the Rational City*; John Fairfield, *The Mysteries of the Great City: Politics of Urban Design 1877-1937* (Columbus: Ohio State University Press, 1995); Richard E. Fogelsong, *Planning the Capitalist City: The Colonial Era to the 1920s* (Princeton: Princeton University Press, 1986); Stanley K. Schultz, *Constructing Urban Culture: American Cities and City Planning, 1800-1920* (Philadelphia, 1989);

Joel Schwartz, *The New York Approach: Robert Moses, Urban Liberals, and Redevelopment of the Inner City* (Columbus: Ohio State University Press, 1993); and Jon C. Teaford, *The Rough Road to Renaissance: Urban Revitalization in America, 1940-1985 (Baltimore: Johns Hopkins University Press, 1990)*.

17.   Herbert Muschamp, "From an Era When Equality Mattered," *New York Times*, Feb. 20, 2000.

18.   For a discussion of these changes in the planning profession, see Frederick J. Adams and Gerald Hodge, "City Planning Instruction in the United States: The Pioneering Days, 1900-1930," *Journal of the American Institute of Planners* 31:1 (Feb. 1965), 43-51; Boyer, *Dreaming the Rational City*; and Michael P. Brooks, "Four Critical Junctures in the History of the Urban Planning Profession," *Journal of the American Planning Association* (Spring 1998), 241-47.

19.   Jane Jacobs, *The Death and Life of Great American Cities* (New York: Vintage Books, 1961), 282, 289.

20.   Julie A. Reuben, "Challenging the Academy in the 1960s: Radical Critiques of the University as a Site of Knowledge Production," Paper presented at the annul meeting of the American Historical Association, Jan. 8, 2000 (quoted with author's permission). See also Reuben, *The Making of the Modern University: Intellectual Transformation and the Marginalization of Morality* (Chicago: University of Chicago Press, 1996).

21.   Paul Davidoff, "Advocacy and Pluralism in Planning," *Journal of the American Institute of Planners* 31:4 (Nov. 1965), 331-38; 336.

22.   Ibid, 332.

23.   See Robert Neuwirth. "Students Take to the Streets at the Pratt Institute Center for Community and Environmental Development," *Metropolis* 17:3 (Oct. 1997), 74-79, 151, 153; "Planners, Heal Thyselves," series of articles on planning education in the *Journal of the American Planning Association* 59:2 (Spring 1993), 139-152; and Jennifer Stern, "Pratt to the Rescue," *Planning* 55:5 (May 1989), 26-28. See also the PICCED Web site at www.picced.org.

24.   "Advocacy Planning Is Alive and Well in Brooklyn," *Planning* 43:1 (Jan. 1977), 20-22; 22.

25.   Ron Shiffman, quoted in Neuwirth. "Students Take to the Streets," 75.

26.   See Brooks, "Four Criticial Junctures"; Paul Davidoff, "Advocacy and Pluralism in Planning," *Journal of the American Institute of Planners* 31:4 (Nov. 1965), 331-338; Marshall M.A. Feldman, "Perloff

Revisited: Reassessing Planning Education in Postmodern Times," *Journal of Planning Education and Research* 13:2 (Winter 1994), 89-103; Harvey S. Perloff, *Education for Planning: City, State, and Regional* (Baltimore, Md.: Johns Hopkins University Press, 1957); Daniel Schaffer, ed., *Two Centuries of American Planning* (Baltimore: Johns Hopkins University Press, 1988); and Mel Scott, *American Planning Since 1980* (Berkeley: University of California Press, 1969).

27.   "Presidents' Fourth of July Declaration on the Civic Responsibility of Higher Education," American Association of Colleges and Universities, 1999 (www.compact.org/resources/)

28.   See "Building the Service-Learning Pyramid: Engaging Campuses, Creating Citizens," Campus Compact Initiative (www.compact.org/service-learning); Stephen Darwall, "Humanities and the Liberal Arts: The Challenge of Public Universities." *LSAmagazine* (The University of Michigan) (Fall 1997): 28-29; Martha C. Nussbaum, *Cultivating Humanity: A Classical Defense of Reform in Liberal Education* (Cambridge, Mass.: Harvard University Press, 1997); "Presidents' Fourth of July Declaration"; Linda J. Sax, "Citizenship Development and the American College Student," in Ehrlich, *Civic Responsibility*, 3-18; and Jane V. Wellman, "Accounting for the Civic Role: Assessment and Accountability Strategies for Civic Education and Institutional Service," in Ehrlich, *Civic Responsibility*, 323-343.

29.   See Center for Community Partnerships, University of Pennsylvania (www.upenn.edu/ccp/) and Center for Greater Philadelphia, University of Pennsylvania (www.upenn.edu/cgp)

30.   City Design Center, College of Architecture and the Arts, The University of Illinois at Chicago (www.uic.edu/aa/cdc/).

31.   Margaret E. Dewar and Claudia B. Isaac, "Learning from Difference: The Potentially Transforming Experience of Community-University Collaboration," *Journal of Planning Education and Research* 17:4 (Summer 1998), 334-347.

32.   See Arts of Citizenship, University of Michigan, (www.artsofcitizenship.umich.edu)

33.   David Scobey, "Putting the Academy in Its Place: Building Bridges Between the University and the Community," The University of Michigan Arts of Citizenship Program, 1999.

34.   Arts of Citizenship, University of Michigan, (www.artsofcitizenship.umich.edu)

35.   Scobey, "Putting the Academy in Its Place."

36.   Center for Democracy and Citizenship, Hubert H. Humphrey Institute of Public Affairs, University of Minnesota (www.publicwork.org).

37.   University of Southern California Environmental Sciences, Policy and Engineering Sustainable Cities Program (www.usc.edu/dept/geography/ESPE)

38.   Marjory Stoneman Douglas, "Communities Face their Slums," *Ladies' Home Journal* (October, 1950), 23, 225-27. See also *Dwelling Conditions in the Two Principal Blighted Areas [Coconut Grove Negro Area and the Central Negro Area], Miami Florida*, Planning Board of the City of Miami and the Slum Clearance Committee of the Dade County Health Department (Miami, 1949). Courtesy of Richter Library Special Collections, University of Miami; Thelma Vernell Anderson Gibson, Forbearance (Homestead, FL: self-published, 2000); Raymond A. Mohl, *South of the South: Jewish Activists and the Civil Rights Movement in Miami, 1945-1960* (Gainesville: University Press of Florida, 2004); NPD 70 Planning brochure for Black Grove, 1969. Courtesy of Richter Library Special Collections; and "Negro Housing in Greater Miami and Dade County," pamphlet. Courtesy of Richter Library Special Collections.

39.   Julie Allen Field with Walter Green, "History of the Black Grove: A Planning Model fro America," Miami Interaction (Coral Gables, FL: University of Miami School of Continuing Education 4:2 (Winter 1973), 25-29.

40.   "Black Grove Spirit," from "Coconut Grove USA Centennial Booklet, 1873-1973." Courtesy of Richter Library Special Collections.

PORTRAITS OF
A COMMUNITY

"Place" roots our existence. It marks our beginning and our end. It gives us identity and shapes our character. It grounds our memories. It reflects where we came from, where we live, where we work, where we meet, where we have been and where we are going. Place brings continuity to human life. It joins past to present, present to future, and us to each other.

Excerpt from Miami, The American Crossroad, by Gregory Bush, pg. 202

On the map: **le 9**, **Cape Canaveral**, **The Everglades**, **Miami**

No other place in the United States is like South Florida. Geologically, it is an afterthought, a late baby that barely managed to lift itself out of the sea that still hungrily laps at its shores. The bedrock of this land is eternally stamped with the firm imprint of the sea. Before modern man arrived, very little dry ground existed in South Florida except for a narrow coastal ridge. The ridge served as the rim of a huge bowl that contained a vast "River of Grass"—the Florida Everglades. In several places along the rocky rim, years of pressure from the Everglades erode the rock, creating small rivers and streams that spilled fresh water into the bays surrounding the southern tip of the peninsula.

Long before any people were living in South Florida, heat-loving plants, animals and insects flourished in the moist semi-tropical climate. Although the top-soil was very thin, organic material accumulated in natural indentations in the rock, forming fertile pockets that spawned hammocks—beautiful subtropical forests filled with a profusion of life.

Human beings, destined to be misnamed Indians, discovered South Florida over 4,000 years ago. Some anthropologists believe that Asian natives may have wandered across the Ice Age bridge between Siberia and Alaska and through the years trekked southward, pulled by the warmth of the sun.

Like primitive people everywhere, South Florida's first humans settled on the banks of rivers. Judging from archaeological remains, one of their principal villages was on the north bank of what is today called the Miami River, the site of the future city of Miami.

These tall, handsome and well-developed people found an easy life in the warm land. The men wore simple breech cloths, and the women fashioned skirts from Spanish moss. Their Garden of Eden, filled with pine and hardwood forest, was home to an abundance of bear, deer and wild fowl. A wild cycad, called comptie (coontie), grew spontaneously in the soil. The people dug up the comptie, ground its large root into flour and made bread. Inexhaustible fresh water bubbled up in the rocky land and even in the salty coastal waters. The sea and the rivers teemed with fish, manatee, turtles, oysters, clams, and conch.

Although no metal and little usable stone could be found in South Florida, the native people created a variety of weapons and tools from the abundant shells. Lashed to a stick, a heavy conch shell became a club, its sharp lip a scraper, its spiral center a pick.

They constructed their homes from cypress logs. Build high off the ground, the platforms were open to the elements except for a roof of palmetto thatch. Early craftsmen also hollowed out sea-worthy, dugout canoes from cypress trees.

The Magic City, by Arva Moore Parks

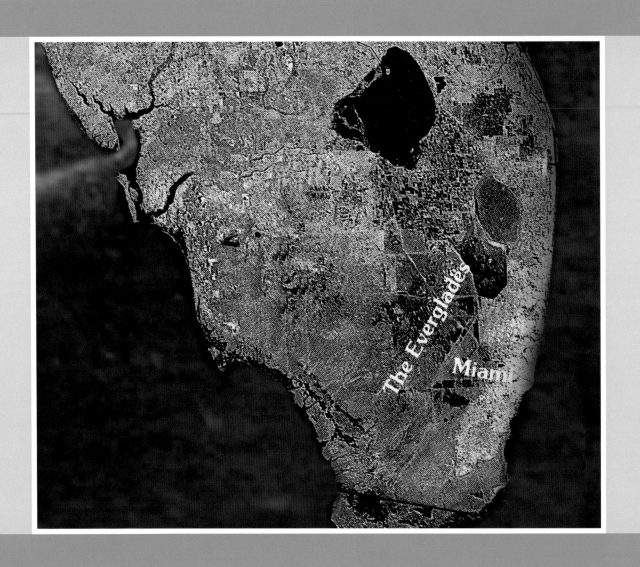

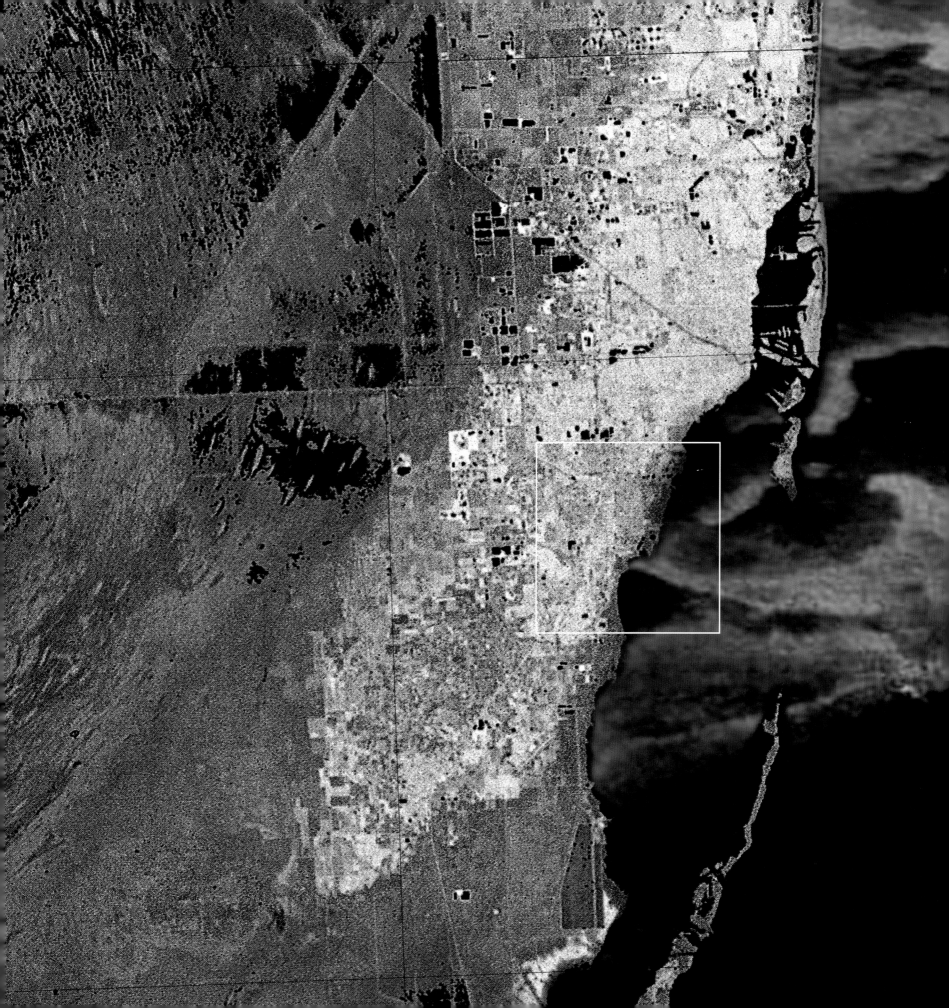

Just as place defines us, we define place and give it meaning. We make, change and write place's history. Those of us who live here today, joined by all who have lived here in the past, have created and continue to recreate this piece of earth we call Miami. Our roots may be elsewhere, but most of us are grafted—one way or another and in varying degrees—into Miami's fertile soil.

Miami's future will flower from this hybrid root system. What will it be like? Should we create a broad framework of multiple identities, or an amalgamation that seeks to promote a larger vision? Who are we anyway? Should we merely see ourselves as Americans in a narrow sense, as people of African heritage, as "Anglos," Cubans, Hispanics? Don't we often overlook our common identity as Miamians?

Living in modern Miami prompts us to be busy, to make and spend money, to protect ourselves and our families. Too often, we define our needs in very personal terms either as individuals or as part of a group. We seem to have lost sight of the larger picture—of ourselves as Miamians, as civic beings interacting with the variety of people who live here with us. We have lost most of the public places that once acted as focal points of community life and have failed to develop new ones.

Thus, Miami continues the struggle to define itself and build a lasting identity. It is easy to see why this has been a daunting task. Most of us, now and in the past, came from someplace else. We often leave our sense of place back home or try to transplant "back home" here. We have destroyed most of our visible past as the wrecking ball of economics beat against continuity. We have allowed others to constantly reinvent us—one trendy, glittery, unreal image after the next.

We have see community spirits soar when teams like the Dolphins, Hurricanes, Panthers and Marlins have championship seasons. We come together in a meaningful way when faced with a tragedy like Hurricane Andrew but the bonding doesn't last.

Will we ever be more than the shifting sands of our beaches, the glow of our brilliant sun and the uncertainty of our raging storms? If we can come together and recognize the fact that we are creating a city unique in American history, we will have built something of lasting value.

Gregory W. Bush

Arva Moore Parks

from Miami, The American Crossroad

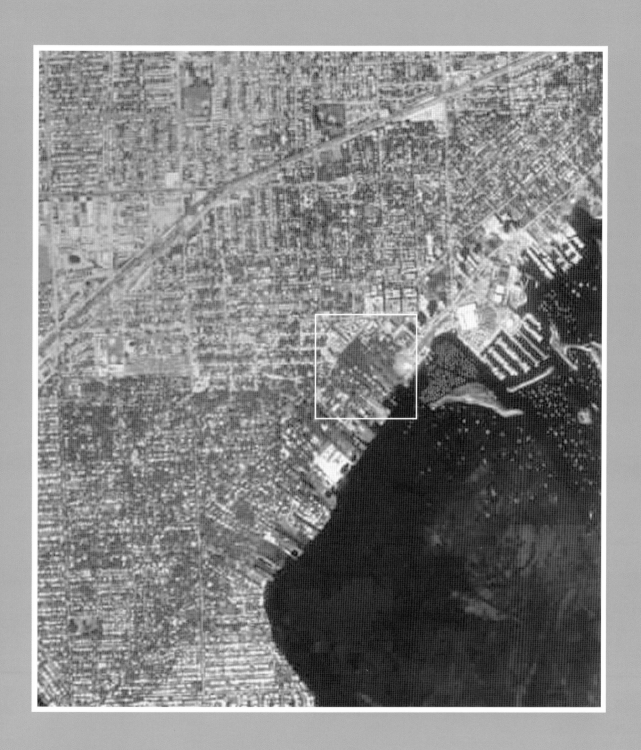

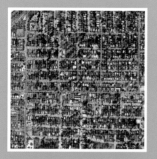

 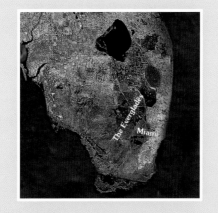 

Oral Histories

Gregory W. Bush
University of Miami School of Arts & Sciences
Department of History

Photo: J.J. Gama-Lobo

IMPACT OF SEGREGATION

My grandfather died before I was born. I remember my grandmother. She was born in the Bahamas. My grandmother looked like any one of you sitting here. Had long, curly hair and she was light skinned. My father was the only one of her children who took her color. And so, looking so much like a white man, he could go anywhere in this town and his children couldn't go. He would go to White Town, and he could go into the drug store. There was a drugstore where the Playhouse is now. Papa could go in that drugstore and come out with sodas or ice cream cones or anything else for his little colored children standing around outside. When we'd go with papa anywhere, and people would say, "Is this your papa? Are you sure this is your papa?" And we'd say, "Yeah, this is our papa." But most people who didn't know, thought he was a white man. He died Christmas of '97 at age ninety-four.
Thelma Anderson Gibson

My father was very independent, and he could not have white bosses over him. I suppose that stems from the fact that when he came to this

country, segregation was very rampant and very harsh. He never told us that but he could not have white bosses over him, even though as a yard man, he had to work for white families, but he knew what he had to do and he didn't have anybody standing over him.
Reverend Austin Cooper

My brother was among the countless in the Grove who were called into service, did time, and came back to a segregated community. There was some bitterness. Some of the soldiers formed organizations, which came into being to do good in the community and to attempt to overcome some of the still present injustices that abounded. Soldiers came back determined that they simply were not going to take it, after have giving their lives, some of whom did surrender their lives-- a couple of the boys from the Grove were killed--to come back and accept the same thing.
Reverend Austin Cooper

An old man, who, first of all, he was shocked that a little black boy would come up there asking for a book of this kind of stature. I supposed that he must have reckoned within himself, or said, "this little Negro boy could come and has the temerity to come in here, knowing that he is not supposed to be here, but to ask for a book like this I have to give it to him." He gave me the book and told me what to do and when to bring it back. I was immobilized by fear, but I sure knew it was a place that we frequented. I went in and explained that my teacher had told me to come there to look for that book, and when he got over his initial shock, and I got over my fear, I think then we came to some understanding, and he gave me the book. I didn't go back because I knew we were not supposed to be there. We had a library at Carver where we got the books that came from the other libraries. I went to Carver, which no longer exists in terms of high school. I went from first right through twelfth, at the school, which sits across the street from which I grew up. It's now George Washington Carver Elementary. But when I was coming along we went from first through twelve, and uh, we had no auditorium. On very cold days, of course the classrooms were not heated, when we had an assembly we would sit along the corridors. It was warmer in the sun, and then it would have been in a cold classroom. Often times we

received the books, which were hand-me-downs from the other schools. The white schools got the brand new textbooks. In spite of that my teachers who knew that they had a responsibility to us in spite of the inequities of the system to educate us. So my teachers always insisted that, never mind the fact that the page is missing from the book, what is important is that you must learn how to read. If you can't read it doesn't matter a damn or not if the book has pages or not pages, if you can't read, you are hurting from the very outset. What is important is you learn how to read. Therefore, when you get a book with all the pages you can read those too. The inequities of the present must be overcome by your determination to rise above. Our teachers who knew that by and large they were dealing with children who came from poor families, instilled in us these two things: you can use your poverty and the lack of materials that are rightly yours as permanent impediments and obstacles in your life, or you can use them as stepping stones to higher things and nobler heights. It rests with you the individual.
Reverend Austin Cooper

Blanche: He would have parties, like the

University of Miami would have parties. Dr. Ashe was the president then. They had parties and if we served at parties, we needed identifications to show why we were coming through the Gables.

Loretta: Yeah, I know they put my nephew in jail. His girl was working at the Sebastian Hotel, and he wanted to pick her up before eight. He was kinda late and he got in trouble for that. That got him put in jail in Coral Gables.

Mother Kent told her that, "Louise, make sure that wherever you work they take out so many pennies. So when you get to be of age, you can get social security." That was the hardest thing momma always said for everybody where she worked to actually want to do the paperwork and do it, and momma said she insisted. She said, "No, you fill out this form and mail it in because Mother Kent said to." Years later, she could collect her social security. A lot of black people weren't told that.
Leona Cooper-Baker Group Interview

LOCAL BUSINESSES

There were a lot of families who had what we

Photo: J.J. Gama-Lobo

called 'mom and pop' stores in the Grove back then. But my most vivid memory is of the Wallace family--because they had the one restaurant on Douglas Road where you could get the best barbecue in town. And then you

Photo: Richard Shepard

had the Dunn's, who had the drugstore. Was where all the children went. You have to remember that in those days we didn't have television. So, the only things you could do was to go to church, to school and on Saturdays to a movie. We could go to the Ace Theater. We'd go to the movies on Saturday, and we could go to the Dew Drop Inn, which was the Dunn's drugstore. On Sunday afternoons, you went to church in the morning. You went to Sunday School at three o'clock, and you went to Young People's Service League at six. The only place you could go in between was to the Dew Drop Inn. The few times you got to go out to dinner, we'd go to the Wallace's Restaurant there. The stores on Grand Avenue were pretty much owned by Jewish people. Izzy's Market was one of the markets there, right next to where the theater was at that time. You had the Toback's, who had another drugstore, and you had Sara Snyder, who had the dry goods store. And then, what we had were beauty shops. There were a lot of barber shops and beauty shops in the Grove. The one family that had a big place on Grand Avenue were the Cashes. The Cash family owned a store right Walt's Laundromat is today. That was the Cash's building. They had a

poolroom one side, a grocery store in the middle and Mrs. Cash had a sewing shop, where she made dresses and that sort of thing. The family lived upstairs. The Carrys had a building, that had the same kind of situation, where Sara Snyder's dry good store was on the side. Her daughter had a beauty shop on the other side. And they lived upstairs over the building. Then there was a meat market that was run by another Jewish family. I do remember the one on Douglas Road, where the Hammersmith family ran the drug--the store on Douglas Road right off of Florida Avenue.
Thelma Anderson Gibson

[The barbershop] was one of the gathering places for the black men. . . There were always bars. There was one called the Pine Inn on Grand Avenue, which was owned by a black man named John Knowles. I think [my father] went there [laughs]. He was friendly with them all. There was some concern, as I recall, in the forties and fifties as whites became owners or had been owners, of how they made the money. At the end of the night, they closed up and left the community with all the problems. They took the money and went into the areas where they lived, and the community was stuck with the problems.
Reverend Austin Cooper

Grand Avenue when I was growing up, was much more prosperous than it is right now. As I said, the owners of the businesses at the time were mostly Jewish families that owned or Orientals. Very few black owned businesses in this community in the late 50's and early 60's. But there were all kinds of businesses. There were several grocery stores, a drug store, the movie theater was actually owned by a black family and still is owned by a black family, the Ace Theater. But when I was growing up that was a theater where you could get in for 15 cents and stay all day or buy popcorn for a nickel and now you have to take twenty dollars just to get into the movies now. There were all kinds of businesses. There were tailors, there were dress shops, teenage restaurants, hardware stores, cleaners.
Yvonne McDonald

Bahamian Promenade

Yvonne MacDonald, President
Coconut Grove Local Development Corporation
Urban Empowerment Corporation

The Bahamian Promenade is an important step in the rebirth of Grand Avenue. Currently, an abandoned group of shops with apartments above, Yvonne McDonald has championed its re-use with collaboration from the City of Miami, and the University of Miami.

The Bahamian Promenade will be re-born as a mixed-use building located on Grand Avenue in the heart of Coconut Grove. The ground level contains three storefront shops that range in size form 500 to 800 square feet and face Grand Avenue. There is on-site parking and public restrooms, in addition to the outdoor patio adjacent to the corner store.

The first apartment is situated on the ground level, to the rear of the retail shops, and is 100% handicapped accessible. The additional four residential untis are located on the second level of the building, acces-sible by two stairways which lead to a covered exterior corridor. Each apartment has one bedroom, one bathroom, a living room and a full kitchen. Additional options include having a private outdoor terrace off of the bedroom or adding a second bedroom to one of the units. All of the residents will also have access to the on-site laundry area on the ground level.

For residents and shopkeepers alike, te Bahamian Promenade is ideally located for both convenient access to all of the amenities of Coconut Grove as well as along the main artery leading form US-1 into the Grove.

Photo: Geneva Farber. Yvonne McDonald, Samina Quraeshi, and Shirley Franco review plans.

Photos: Yvonne McDonald

Drawing by Koroglu Associates

The Tables are Turned

Sanjeev Chatterjee
University of Miami School of Communication

Photography and Video students from the
School of Communication and the Art
Department shared ideas and images with a full
range of people and places in the community.
Prints of photographs were given to their sub-
jects to encourage this exchange. The student's
video documentary had its premier on Grand
Avenue in May of 2000.

nd what about the community? Above all, we e outsiders, not only because we are geo-aphically separated, but also because we are parate historically and economically. Our iny cameras bear blatant evidence of the iture of this relationship. The madman at the orner who tends to his self-proclaimed golf ourse shouts obscenities at my students for ying to point the camera at him. At least he is onest. Once in a while someone offers to sell rugs to us, or proposes to be interviewed for 25.

hen I ask my students about this place, ough, they only speak of the colorfulness, the armth, the welcome, the sense of everybody iowing everybody that emanatess from being the West Grove. What can we do as

filmakers? The architects are building a house, something tha will stay with the community for years to come. so I ask my students, are we here merely to hone our skills?

"No. I don't think that we are making this documentary merely to practice our skills, although that is certainly one important aspect of it. In addition to learning and growing in the field of documentary and video production, this project has provided us with the opportunity to educate people about Coconut Grove. Our job has been to act as an extension to the audience, eyes and ears, so that they can see and hear for themselves the current situation in West Coconut Grove."

Joseph 'Rainey' Rucker

"Yes, we were here to learn how to work together to produce a documentary as a team. We wanted to learn how the world of documentary filmmaking worked, and produce something better than any of us could produce alone. Now we all have opinions about the area and what should be done to help it prosper. Now we enjoy visiting the community. Now we care. Now we care what this video does once we are finished. Now we care about what we have learned from doing this project on a social community level, and not just a classroom level."

Theresa Santelli

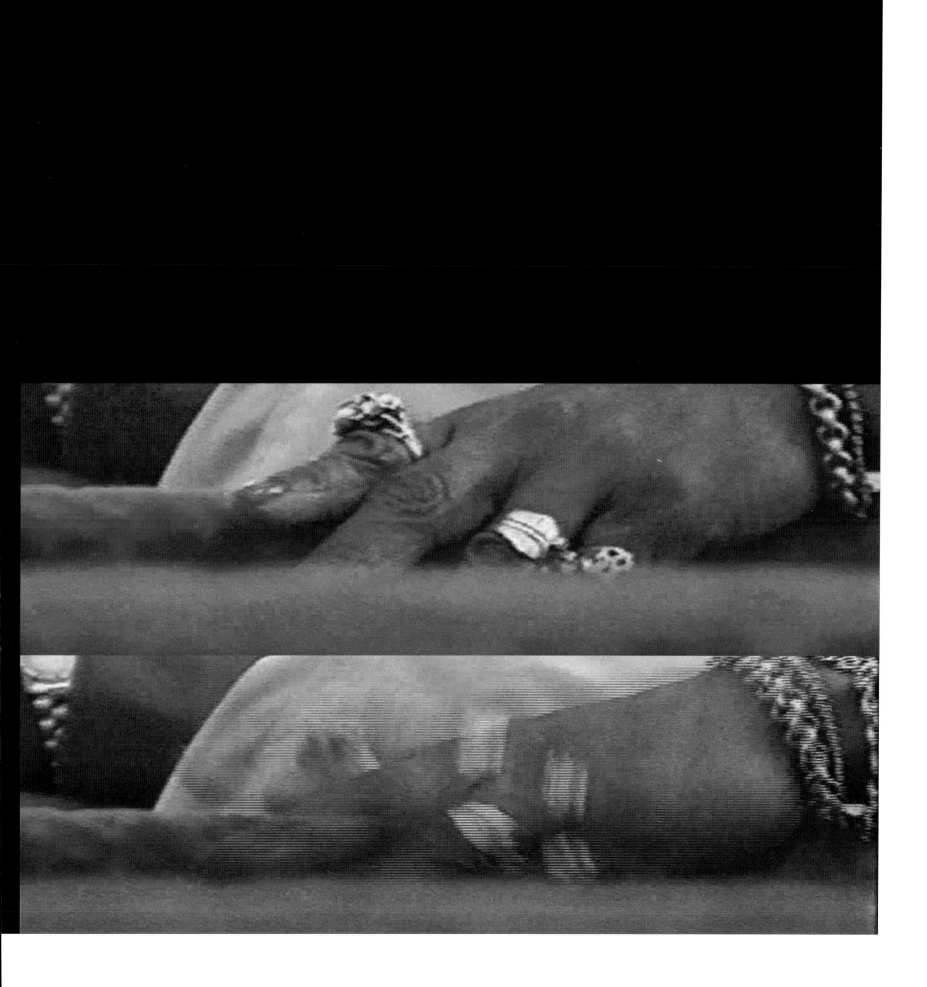

Oral Histories

Gregory W. Bush
University of Miami School of Arts & Sciences
Department of History

Photo: Miranda Mulligan

RELATIONSHIP TO WHITE FAMILIES

Certainly I used to hear the old people talk about the times when the Klan would parade through Coconut Grove. However, even then the community many times was protected by whites for whom they worked, who may have. . .heard that the Klan was going to be parading in the Grove at certain times. They would tell their employees who lived in the Grove, so people were able to prepare for it. There had to be a network because very few people had telephones. Everything was done by word of mouth.
Reverend Austin Cooper

When my father would bring home grape fruits that the Gamas would give him, or mangoes and what not, he would share that fruit all around this neighborhood [during the Depression].
Vernika Silva

TERROR OF KKK

Everybody was the type that you could talk to, or they would stop and talk with you. It was just those individuals that I thought lived far out, [the] Ku Klux Klan and all that. I remember one

Saturday night. I remember we were coming home and my father had just gone to the ice cream parlor and bought us some ice cream. I think I was about eight years old, and I saw all the individuals dressed in white, some were walking and some were on horses. I stood up and watched them because they didn't bother you unless you bothered them…I remember people hiding…They always had the covering and what not and did what you expected them. I think that was in part because some of the individuals that lived in this area they claimed that someone went down to the park and took them and killed them. There was never evidence of what happened.
Vernika Silva

Blanche: In Allendale, we went to those beaches because they wasn't particularly populated like Miami…but this was after the Ku Klux. (laughs) This was after the Ku Klux and they used to have signs up.

Loretta: You had time to look and read and run. (laughs) I know when the Ku Klux came to Mr. Stone…(commotion)…

Blanche: I remember when they came to the park right there.

Loretta: They come to him.

Blanche: My daddy had a shotgun with him. He took that 'cause he took me and my brother to see the Ku Kluxes, and we had never seen 'em.

Loretta: Boy, did you see that. They come to get him. I'll tell you this little story when my daddy was here. Stone come from the Bahamas, but he come to Key West. First they come to Key West then they come here. Anyway, this white girl liked Mr. Stone…and Mr. Stone must've liked her too. He sent a note to her…and they find out he wrote to her. Now, Mr. Stone and her used to stay together. They take the note from her, but he didn't have no name. They take the note from her and they went to him. They said, "Nigger, is this you." He said, "Oh yeah…I can't read or write." He said, "Nigger, you know you can read and write 'cause everybody from the Bahamas could. Right here!" He said, "I can't read or write." That's the only thing that saved him. Then they come to papa, and they say, "I know you know." She said, "I know he can't read or write." That's a good thing he say that 'cause they was gonna lynch him!

Loretta: When I come here, they used to parade every week.

Loretta: That's right. Grandmama come for one year, and then she look and see their leader and the cross burnin' and the people yellin'...she said, "Carry me back home, and I'll go home and smoke a cigarette. I can't live here." Really, she lived here until she died.

Interviewer: What day of the week did they parade? Did they have a regular schedule?

Blanche: Weekends, mostly.

Interviewer: Weekends?

Loretta: Yeah. You could go out your house and see the parade.

Ellen: They'd do it more around the election.

Interviewer: Is that right? You remember?

Ellen: Yeah, I remember once there right across of Grand before the election.

Loretta: You remember where they were gonna take Mr. Hicks?

Interviewer: Oh yeah, I remember that...back in 1920, 1921 or something.

Loretta: I remember Mr. Hicks. They got out of church...him and his brother built my church...he went down to Key West to a convention, and he was preaching and he telling 'em, "Keep giving your children a good education." That's so they can get a good job, not maiding and washing and stuff like that. And the Ku Klux go over there and called Coconut Grove Ku Klux, and told them what he was saying, trying to keep them out of the kitchen and not washing dishes. You know what I'm talking about! That night around six o'clock one carload had come to his house, and his little boy Alfonso who was eleven years old, and the man come to the door and knocked. He said, "Is your daddy here?" He say yes. He said, "Tell him that somebody in the car want to see him." So he ran and said, "Daddy, there's a man out in the car want to see you." Well, he said it was a man but he didn't know it was anybody from the Ku Klux or anything like that, and he went around. Jesse got to the door, they opened it, and they take his arms and a hood over his head and throw him in the car and speed off.

Interviewer: You saw that? Or you heard the story?

Loretta: No, I didn't see it. That's what his son telling my daddy. He said, "Momma, a car let a man take my daddy off." Oh, and there was a riot. If it hadn't been for Mr. Peacock, they was gonna kill him.

Interviewer: What do you remember about that afterwards?

Loretta: Well, they go with him and carry him

down to a place called Fort Lonesome. That's down there...what's the name of it? I remember...and all the boys and them getting mad you know. We're throwing rocks at the cars and everything, and there was gonna be a riot. So my daddy that night ran down to a boat coming from the Bahamas, and he ran down there to get something. Coming back, we wasn't living here. We lived with Mr. Rice on 8th Street between 22nd and 27th Avenue. When he get to the bridge, he see all these people and everybody had guns and everything. Then he said that

Photo: Richard Shepard

something bad was happening in Coconut Grove. He said, "Every time I come to a bridge, everyone have a gun!" Papa was on a bicycle, and he said, "Nigger, get down here! Are you going to Coconut Grove?" Papa said, "No, I don't live there. I live with Richard Rice. Where he live, I live." So he said, "You sure you ain't going down there?" He said, "No!" So when he come home, he said, "Something bad happening!" So one man know papa in the crowd, and he say, "Oh no, that's a good nigger! I know him." He said, "I'll take you across to the other side." And he did. He said, "Don't bother him. He's good." And papa come home and papa tell us there's something bad happening. Well, all Grand Avenue...all the white cars that passed they was throwing rocks. **Interviewer:** White people's cars? Throwing rocks!

Loretta: Yeah...no, the black were throwing at the white... 'cause they couldn't find him. He looked for him...couldn't find him nowhere. Now, the next morning they find him...a white lady find him and bring him home. Now, I see this. All his shoulder is there, but all over his body where you could see the whip you could see the bone. Now I see that. He say, "Nigger, you got twenty four hours to get out!" And all

the Ku Klux in the neighborhood was there. That happened on Saturday, and he was supposed to leave on Sunday. Pop and them got a boat, and got everything prepared, and carry him down there. Mister...oh Lord, when I look at that I was a young girl. All over his body, they cut him, all over his face. The only thing save him, he was a Masonic. Mr. Peacock...he was there. Man, he put up his sign, his distress sign. Mr. Peacock was one. He said, "Don't put another cut on him! Leave him!" They was gonna kill him. They leave him there to die. All night he went, he didn't know where he was. He had to crawl on his hands and feet until he see someone that morning. Everybody was panicked in the Grove. They was gonna get a gun...murder in white town. (passing motor drowns out sound) Mr. Peacock run down there and tell the boys, "Now listen!" 'Cause he was one too! 'Cause he tell papa everything. He say...(passing motor drowns out sound)...he was not dead, 'cause he was different. He didn't whip him. He tell him say that after he put that sign up, the sign of distress, the Mason sign. He say don't put another cut on him, and that's what saved him. That morning, when he saw the sun, he didn't know it was east or west.

The white lady pick him up and brought him home. Our child was free, yeah.
Leona Cooper-Baker Group Interview

Photo: Richard Shepard

Behind the Scenes in Coconut Grove

Michael Carlebach
University of Miami School of Arts & Sciences
Department of Art & Art History

Photo: Nic DeGracia

This project introduced students to the methods and meanings of documentary photography. The opportunity to participate in an interdisciplinary effort to document the physical and cultural environments of West Coconut Grove, a black community not far from the University seemed ideally suited to this purpose. Our principal objective was to provide strong black and white portraits of the citizens of the West Grove. Students took part in public exhibitions of work produced. This was a revelation: students at the University of Miami rarely, if ever, get to see what goes on outside their own areas of concentration. My students vowed to continue working there. This is reason enough, it seems to me, to explore ways to institutionalize interdisicplinary learning.

Photo: Miranda Mulligan

Photo: Michael Carlebach

KEBO: The Rediscovery of a Neighborhood

Lelen Bourgoignie-Robert
University of Miami School of Communication

Photo: Kamal Farah

The colors, textures, sentiments and relationships present throughout the community, were, in fact, the subject of the documentary. We sought to communicate the unique atmosphere of the West Grove in order to show that this atmosphere is the function of both the physical environment and the people who live there. The experience gave us insight into the lives and routines of a neighborhood trying to regain both its stature and its reputation. We entered the area free from any preconceptions, and thus began absorbing the character and charm present. After numerous visits we began to take pictures of the community as it was revealed to us.

Photo: Amanda Kerr

Photo: Miranda Mulligan

Photo: Kamal Farah

Virrick Park

Will Johnson, President
Virrick Park Committee

Six years ago, before Miami-Dade County successfully promoted and the people passed the "Safe Neighborhoods Park Bond Issue," to fund the revitalization of the City and County's flagging park systems, a group of Groveites and friends began meeting about the conditions at Virrick Park. There was not much fan-fare. There was not much of a plan. There was only a dream that one day Virrick Park would live up to expectations of those who had originally founded it.

Mrs. Elizabeth L. Virrick, founded the Coconut Grove Citizens Committee for Slum Clearance in 1948. She later teamed with Reverend Theodore R. Gibson, Rector, Christ Episcopal Church and Secretary of the Coconut Grove Ministerial Alliance, members of the City Commission and Mayor, Robert King High, to purchase land between Day Avenue, Plaza Street, Hibiscus Street and Oak Avenue, for the creation of a park. Mrs. Virrick and Rev. Gibson, who later served as a City Commissioner, knew that just clearing away dilapidated houses and building sewers and side walks was not all there was to building a neighborhood. They realized that parks are the heart and soul of communities. And, on Saturday, June 15, at 2 p.m., in 1963, Virrick Park was dedicated.

For years the park thrived, providing the community with green-space to play in, buildings to meet in and later a pool to wile away hot afternoons in. But, as the City fell on financial hard times and suffered through one political leadership crisis after another, parks, never a high priority in the first place, became even a lower priority. In the City, maintenance and management of all its parks were neglected with devastating results.

After years of physical and financial neglect, Virrick Park slipped from being a source of community pride, to being a source of neighborhood embarrassment. At the point where the park had hit absolute rock-bottom, buildings falling apart, homeless people sleeping of the benches, rampant drug dealing and use and blatant open prostitution, a group of citizens decided to take the park back. In the spirit of Mrs. Virrick's and Rev. Gibson's "Slum Clearance Committee," the Virrick Park Committee was born. That was about six-years ago, but, the Committee can trace its linage back to 1963. The timing was providential. The Committee, with assistance from the original architect of the 1963 creation, Mr. Kenneth Treister, quickly became energized and organized.

Ms. Thelma Edwards, an original founder of the present-day, Virrick Park Committee, and the first Neighborhood Enhancement Team, Administrator for the West Grove recalls: "We were ahead of the game when the Safe Neighborhoods Bond issue passed. We had long in place, organization, architecture and design and community consensus when the bond committee started to look at projects to fund. This enabled Virrick Park to receive some of the first money awarded from the bond issue." The money awarded was not enough to complete even the first phase of the project to the standards set by the Committee, however. Some in City government urged and advised the Committee to accept what they were given and just build something. Out of that urging grew the Committee's rallying cry, which still drives them today, "a first class facility or no facility." Along the way the Committee/Coconut Grove citizens have gained the respect and admiration of City government. The City has become powerful boosters, supporters and believers in the vision that the Committee has for Virrick Park. They no longer doubt or advise the community to "just build something." They now share and push the vision of a "first class facility," in Virrick Park.

Phase one is complete and with the help of its partners, the University of Miami, United Way, Boys & Girls Club, Coconut Grove Cares, The BarnYard, The James L. Knight Foundation, The City of Miami and the Miami-Dade County, the Committee has set sail to complete Phase II. Phase II will house a full service branch of the Miami-Dade Library, Music Room, Computer Lab/Class Rooms, Crafts Room, and Cooking Lab.

United Way Work-A-Thon brought 3000 volunteers to rebuild Virrick Park.

Photos: Richard Shepard

President of the University of Miami, Donna Shalala lends a hand.

79

What is Virrick Park?: What will its life be?
What will be its heart and soul?

Concrete and mortar.
Steel and aluminum.
Imported sand-stone and broken ceramic
 tiles.
Copper wires and plastic conduits.
Sod, soil and trees.
City and County government working
 together for the good of its citizenry.
Thousands of hours of paid and volunteer
 labor.
An architect's historically-guided-vision.
A community's determination not to set
 tle for less -- this time.
A community's shared dream.

Twelve answers to the question: "What is
Virrick Park?"

The January breeze blowing through the
 oak trees.
A couple huddled close together, wrapped
 in a blanket, sitting on a cold tile bench
 on a February night.
A March Easter Egg hunt.
A family re-union party in April.
Labor Day Picnics in late May.
A play on the Community Center/Gym
 stage in June.
The splashing sound of people enjoying
 the pool on a hot July evening.
The squeaky shoe sounds of mid-night
 basketball in August.
The sweet sounds of church choirs enter
 taining and inspiring on the out-door

stage in September.
The dizzying, delightful array of smells as
 food vendors prepare lunch for an
 October festival.
A noisy, never-ending, nasty, night of
 Rapp/Rock/Blues/Jazz in November.
Christmas lights strung from pillar to post
 with a large decorated tree as a center-
 piece in December.

Sixteen answers to the question: "What will be
the life of Virrick Park?"

People, people, people.
People everywhere.
People all over the place.
People every day.
People every hour.
People of every color, every description,
 every voice.
People who come to play.
People who come to work.
People who come to volunteer.
People who come to meetings.
People who come to entertain.
People who come to be entertained.
People who have just begun their life's
 run.
People in the middle of life's trials.
People, wise and seasoned by long-years
 on the path.
Mostly and mainly, plain ole community
 folks.

The one answer to the question: "What will be
the heart and soul of Virrick Park?"

Will Johnson

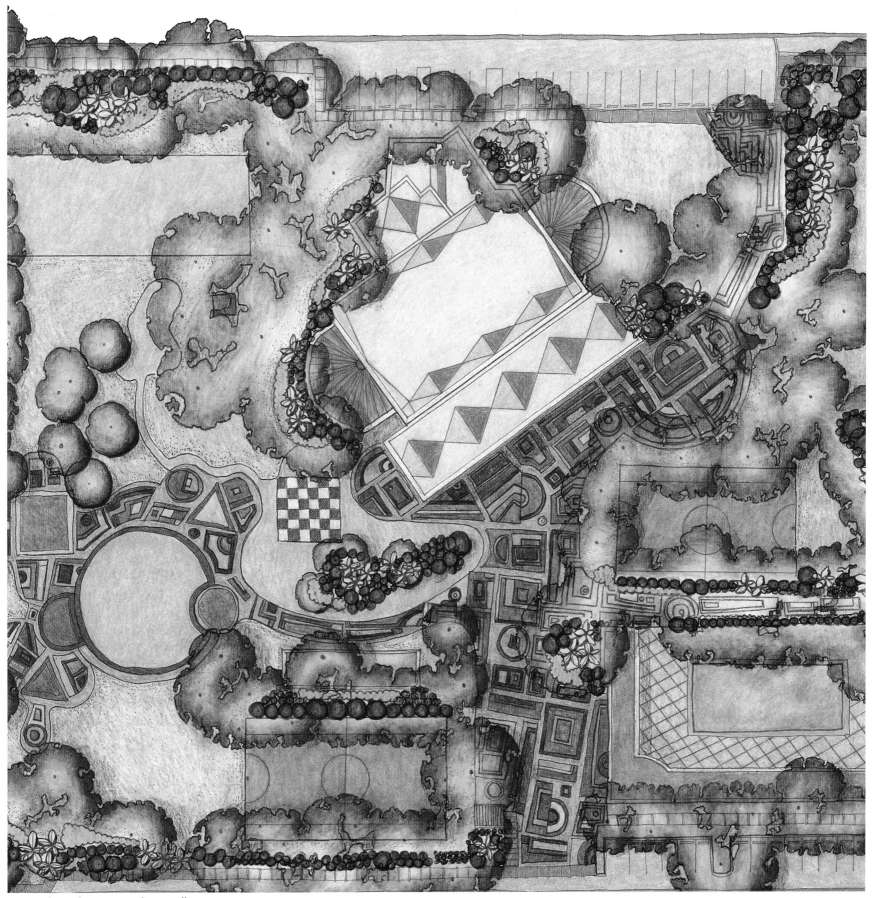

Drawing by Stephanie Wyn Graham-Bradley

INTERVENTIONS

...HE CONSTRUCTION PROCESS EVEN AT TH...
...HASE. THE PROJECT IS SO SMALL IT REALLY...
...ASY TO UNDERSTAND. JODI AND I STARTED...
...HE DAY NAILING WHICHEVER JOISTS...
...ARRIED TWO PIECES OF WOOD.
...S OF TODAY THE CONCRETE HAS...
...ET TO BE POURED. APPARENTLY,...
...HE PLANS DID NOT CALL FOR LIGHTNING...
...DS IN THE PILINGS, SO THE ELECTRICAL PL...
...VE TO BE REVISED + RESUBMITTED.
...ARIO ARRIVED AT THE SITE WITH DRAWIN...
...OR ARMANDO IN ORDER TO BETTER EXP...
...HE ELEVATIONS + THEIR OPENINGS - SO...
...E WALLS CAN START TO BE BUILT.
...DELIVERY OF PLYWOOD SHEETS FOR THE...
...+ SMALLER PIECES OF WOOD +...

Gregory W. Bush
University of Miami School of Arts & Sciences
Department of History

ROLE OF REVEREND THEODORE GIBSON

[Father Gibson] came to my home parish, which is Christ's Church in Coconut Grove, when I as twelve years old. He came October first, nineteen forty-five. Father Gibson grew up in Overtown. I remember his first Sunday there. I was just a boy, but I remember it very well. Now, I was in his first confirmation class. He was very demanding. He demanded always of you your best, not somebody else's best, but your best. He was not one to settle for shiftlessness, chatter, and badly done things. He was a stickler for time. He believed in you as a person. He believed that you could be whatever you set out to be, but you had to have a sense of determination yourself. Others could help you, but it had to begin with you. He had grown up in it. Conditions were even worse when he grew up than when I grew up, because he could remember the Klan riding through Overtown or colortown, as we called it, when he was a boy. *Reverend Austin Cooper*

He could fight you and love you at the same time. He was a man of great vision for the community, he always saw things as they were, but

Historical photography courtesy of Arva Moore Parks

he always saw things as they could be. Who said some men say things as they are and ask why I dream of things as they never were, and ask why not? That was father Gibson. He was always asking why not? He fought whites over racial injustices, every ounce of his being, but he never stooped low enough to hate whites. I used to be his sidekick, and I would go to meetings with Father Gibson at night, to meetings of the (Slum) Committee it was called. He was also president of NAACP, I would go to NAACP meetings with him at night, as a boy. Many times, I didn't have the foggiest notion what those adults were talking about, but I knew they were talking about freedom. I knew they were talking about something that will make this community better. I believe there was some meeting up in what we called the village.
Reverend Austin Cooper

A miniature McCarthy Committee wanted the names of the Miami NAACP members [was] so that they could bring retribution against the blacks who [were] members, the schoolteachers, and the white members of NAACP, so that they could cause them economic problems. Too many whites who were supporters but who

couldn't let it be known, for obvious reasons. So father Gibson almost went to jail protecting these people, he used the constitutional right to association. Even then, he was only [unintelligible] in a five-four decision, which means it could have gone the other way against him. That was 1963 when the court handed down this decision.
Reverend *Austin Cooper*

He was strictly a civil rights man, much to the dismay of many in the hierarchy of the Episcopal Church, but he felt he had a mission and a calling to, prophetic mission, to do something to change the plot and plight of his people. He firmly believed that education was to empower you to do good for others, and he lived and died by that code, that philosophy.
Reverend Austin Cooper

And as the result of that, I remember when Father Gibson worked with the slum clearance, some of the members of his parish were very...there was a conflict at that time because some of the members of his church owned some of the houses that were cleared. . . Ellen: They were having to spend the money to put the

Historical photograph of Elizabeth Virrick courtesy of Arva Moore Parks

toilets in and they didn't have the money. It probably cost more to put a toilet in those houses than they were getting for rent, and they didn't really do that for a long time.

Leona: Father Gibson done that, but some of the members didn't like that.

Leona Cooper-Baker Group Interview

ROLE OF ELIZABETH VIRRICK

Mrs. Virrick deeded this park to the city. These used to be houses out here in this compound -- her property. From my understanding, this building was erected to satisfy the needs of West Grovites and there was no racial connotation. The primary purpose of the mushroom design is that years ago, if you saw the little TV box out there, was to have families come out to the park who could not afford to have a TV or air-conditioning. They would get together and see programs like boxing matches or basketball games. Many outdoor activities took place here on Sundays so that kids could play and not have to stay in the house.

Park Manager, Ron Lopez

Photo: Richard Shepard

Celebrating Children and the Arts

Jennifer Jones
Jones Consulting

A new and unique elementary charter school will soon open its doors to parents in Miami-Dade County. The Theodore R. and Thelma A. Gibson Charter School will offer a curriculum in which traditional subject areas — math, science, history, social studies and language — are taught through the arts.

Photo: Richard Shepard

MISSION AND BACKGROUND

The mission of The Gibson School is to promote self-expression, creative problem-solving, and hands-on exploration among children. To achieve its mission, The Gibson School will offer an environment in which the study of academic subjects is merged with an exploration of artistic disciplines, including painting, sculpture, dance, music and theatre. Themes will guide instruction, and special emphasis will be given to the Caribbean and African cultural influences prevalent among residents of the West Grove, where the school is located. The Gibson School is the brainchild of Thelma Gibson, a prominent community leader in Coconut Grove as well as Greater Miami and widow of the late Canon Theodore R. Gibson, who served on the Miami City Commission and was active in the Civil Rights Movement. The Gibson Fund has for twenty years worked to bridge the divide between ethnic communities in Miami through various projects as well as the annual sponsorship of a "Unity Dinner" in which it honors three outstanding Dade citizens who have contributed to unity in our region.

THE SCHOOL

In its first year of operation, the Gibson School will enroll a maximum of 200 students in kindergarten through second grade. Each year, the school will expand upwards and increase the number of classes offered in each grade. Eventually, founders of the school hope to offer preschool through 8th grade. Class sizes will be small, with a maximum of 25 students per teacher. The school will open with nine teachers and a principal.

CURRICULUM

The Gibson School recognizes the power of the arts in intellectual development. Creation is itself an intellectual journey that requires interdisciplinary methods, including those associated with science, math, language, social studies, and history. Art offers the opportunity for student self-direction and self-awareness. Art offers the ultimate opportunity for differentiated learning, so that children of varied levels of readiness can engage a similar topic each through his/her own set of strengths and interests. Finally, art provides students, teachers, and parents with a clearly measurable process and product; growth in all learning domains can be seen with more clarity, enabling those held

Photo: Richard Shepard

accountable for student performance to demonstrate the complexity and non-linearity of human development.

The Gibson School program design has evolved primarily from three influences: the use of the environment as curriculum emphasized by Reggio Emilia schools in northern Italy; the hands-on focus of the Montessori model; and the rich arts curriculum of the internationally-renowned Waldorf School.

RELATIONSHIP WITH COMMUNITY

The curriculum, as well as the building, will embrace community members. Teachers will involve local artists in student activities, fostering mentorships and community outreach. The work of both students and local artists will be exhibited throughout the school. With its doors open to the community and with an ongoing series of events that invite community participation and input, the Gibson School not only will provide enrichment for society, but will also offer its students real opportunities to engage the public through artistic expression and interpretation. Children are, in large part, voiceless in the art world, and yet their works carry important insights about human development, perspective and interpretation. There is a need to educate the community about children's art and its value in relation to human development, to provide a greater number of children with opportunities to participate in the world of the arts, and to foster mentoring relationships between children and the artists of our region.

INTERVIEW WITH THELMA ANDERSON GIBSON

Thelma Anderson Gibson has lived in Coconut Grove for over seven decades. She was born in the village in 1926, but traces her link to the community back to 1887, when her grandfather, one of several Bahamian immigrants to help create the settlement, arrived there.

She has seen Coconut Grove evolve over the years from "Colored Town" and "White town" – divisions created during segregation. Today, the area is still divided. This time, though, the separation is based on economics. Despite the affluence that has sprung up around it, the West Grove, still known for its rich Bahamian heritage, remains a pocket of poverty.

92

Community leaders and independent organizations, such as the university of Miami, have collaborated on several efforts to address some of the problems in the West Grove. Housing development and healthcare are key considerations in the community, where one in every four residents earn $12,000 or less annually.

Ms. Anderson Gibson, a trustee of the University of Miami, has worked with the institution's nursing and architecture schools to address these issues. Her late husband, Theodore R. Gibson, was a City of Miami commissioner, who in the 1940s, worked to help pass ordinances that brought running water, indoor plumbing and other infrastructure to the community. Today, Ms. Anderson Gibson's latest efforts include plans for a charter school on Grand Avenue. Here, she discusses the University of Miami's community involvement and her hopes for the West Grove.

You have known this neighborhood all your life. How would you describe the quality of community life now as opposed to earlier periods?

So much has happened to improve conditions, and yet there are so many things that are still the same in many areas. There are still a lot of poor people around. The middle class has moved out pretty much, but because you have people like the University of Miami School of Architecture coming in, a lot of things have started happening. The students did a lot. They came up with plans for the Grove to see how it could change, and they did a lot of designs for our school, as well as for housing. It has changed for the better.

What hopes and fears do you have for this community's future?

I'm hoping that we will be able to see change take place to the point that we will have some African-Americans serving as developers, so that we will always be able to have some of the Bahamian flavor. One of the things that I'm almost insisting on with our school is that we have the Bahamian flavor with the Gibson School. And that's why I want to build a "wow" kind of school so that people will want to come and see what we're doing down here and to be able to keep some of what our fore parents brought here.

Everything has changed. If we are not careful, and if we don't do some-

Drawing by Derrick Smith

thing about it, you're not ever going to know that Bahamians were here. I'm hoping that we're going to be able to keep some of that flavor here in the little block that is pretty much owned by black folk in the Grove. In their designs, developers are naming their buildings by islands in the Bahamas, but I don't think that African-Americans will be able to stay in them.

Still, I'm trying to encourage GUTS (Grovites United to Survive, an entrepreneurial group) at this point to do some developing on our own and do some affordable housing on the land that we own in the Grove. Whatever land we acquire, we're hoping to do some affordable housing, perhaps some condos and some rental. [We'll] make it affordable so that we can ensure that some African-Americans will be able to come back.

You want to know my dream? My dream is that we will be able to get some of these black football players and basketball players who become instant millionaires to come in here and start buying some of these apartments and condos in West Coconut Grove in the black community. If just ten of those players decided to put just one million of all those millions that they get into this community, imagine what could happen

down here. We could really have a place where everybody would want to come.

My dream is to have people understand that this is the highest piece of land in Coconut Grove. We don't have flooding down here. We're also fifteen minutes away from almost everywhere in Dade County – only twenty minutes to Miami Beach; twelve minutes to the airport; ten minutes to downtown Miami; twenty minutes down to Homestead or the south area. This is more central than anything else.

My dream is to have somebody wake up and see that they could sell this whole area. I don't mind gentrification so much. I'm not afraid of gentrification. I think if you get the right mixture of people, everything would be well, but we've got to help some of these rich blacks to understand that they could invest in our communities.

You said that African-Americans could not live in the new property that is being developed in Coconut Grove. Is it because the new property is priced beyond their means?

93

Yes, of course...If you go down Grand Avenue, all the buildings you see that are colored gold at the bottom with beige at the top have been bought up by a group of developers. They're coming in and they already have their plans for what they're going to do, starting with Margaret Street, down to Hibiscus. Their places are going to be running in the price range of $200,000 to $250,000. The average person who makes less than $25,000 or $35,000 will not be able to live here. They're going to be bringing people in here who can afford to live in those apartments – and they're not going to be us. And I don't want all blacks. I want a good mixture and a good feeling that some of the young blacks who lived here could afford to come back.

What impact do you feel the University of Miami's work in Coconut Grove has had on the neighborhood?

I think it's been a great deal of help, because not only did we work with the architect students, we had the nursing students who came out. In the past two semesters, we had twenty nursing students out here, and they were able to go into the homes and visit with clients. They were able to get people into healthcare, get them into doctors' offices, into hospitals, into treatment centers. They were able to go in and take blood pressures and do some things the Public Health Department used to do, but are no longer doing. We had these nursing students and they have come in and they have done this. The community is very excited about this. We really feel the university has come in and helped a great deal. When the School of Architecture students were in there helping to make designs, they helped with the streetscaping. They were very helpful and I think that people have benefited from that.

What were the successes of this effort in recent years?

I think it has been very, very successful in that they have been able to do studies and then do something about them. They got the students to help build a house. They continued to try to get houses built, trying to get people to own their own homes. To me, that's been very helpful. They have, of course, recruited in the meantime to get students to come to the school. I think more and more students are beginning to feel that they can go to University of Miami and that's it our school. They're in the community. Before, it was them over there and us over here. But now, I think that they're beginning to get people to want to go to the University of Miami.

[Grove students] want to stay home. While they think they mightn't be able to afford attending the University of Miami, the more they see these students coming here, the more they learn about scholarships and the fact that they can get some help. More and more we have students who want to go there because they see what could happen in the community with the university helping.

Have there been failures in the university's community efforts in recent years?

It's hard to define and see what failures there have been, in that you don't know what's going to happen in the future with the studies that they've done. They've had a lot of charrettes and they've done a lot things in the community, working with the community.

I'm just hoping that in the future these things would continue to go on. The only failure I would see is if they stopped coming in. If they stopped helping or they just abruptly cut off everything that's been coming in here and not have their presence felt – that, to me, would be a great failure.

But so far things are going well?

I think so far things have gone very well. I'm pleased. I don't know if everybody can say that, but unless you've been here and know what's happened, it's kind of hard to see progress. To a lot of people, things still look the same, but we know that things are happening.

Most people want to see something happen on Grand Avenue or on Douglas Road, but there are houses going up on the inside, so that the people who live there are better off. They're beginning to own their own homes, see the need for keeping them up and keeping the surroundings clean and that sort of thing. I think it's been a great improvement.

And the university has contributed to that?

I think so. In a way, they have been very helpful, in that they have been able to continue to have meetings with the community and show them that things could be better and that dreams could come true.

What were the impediments to greater effectiveness?

Always money. It's always that we do not have enough money to do what needs to be done. Unfortunately, while we were working with the Knight Foundation and hoping that they would give us funding, they decided to [fund] Overtown instead of Coconut Grove. The need in Overtown is much greater.

Our little section is so small, people see the larger thing when they look at Overtown or these areas with a lot of people. We only have three or four thousand black people in West Coconut Grove, so they look at it as a small area.

Then, you go down to the South Grove and see all the wealth. You go to the North Grove and see all the wealth. They forget that this little pocket remains with all these poor people still needing help.

It's harder to get help because they think that people around us should help. They think that we shouldn't have to go to anybody else because there's enough wealth within in the community, even though it's not our direct community.

What they don't understand is that most of these people who drive through here don't even look at us. They don't even look at the poverty. They don't even look to see how you can tell from McDonald [Street] when you've gone into the black community. They just want to get through here and get down south or get through here and get up north and that's all. They don't always understand what's happening. People will tell you it looks better when you cross Douglas [Road] and see all the buildings that are going on down there on the north side...But people don't look on the south side. They just look at all this stuff that's going on in the north side and say how good things are.

Has the university been helpful in organizing the Gibson School?

Not really. Not really. They were helpful in helping get designs and talked about how it could be done, but they haven't given us a dime. I hate to say it, but they have not really...I guess in a way they have been helpful, in that they have come in and tried to help do the designs for us, but they didn't go any further than that. We have talked to the School of Education. They talked with us about the curriculum.

However, when you talk about help – as far as helping to get a building done and that kind of stuff – we have not had that kind of help...It could be that they may not know that that's the kind of help that we need. I'm not being critical, because I have not asked for that kind of help. It's probably our fault that we have not asked for help.

Has the university helped with the health initiative?

Yes, it helped with the health initiative. The nursing students are coming in and they're able to go into the community and help us. We only have two full-time staff and three part-time outreach workers. When the students come in, they give us that many more people who can go out and help to educate and help clients feel that they have somebody who cares about them.

While we don't want to be a health department, we do want to have people know that we are out there trying to help and to educate and prevent. I think you can teach people the importance of prevention, and the importance of not getting HIV and being left with AIDS. We give out condoms right and left because we just want people to know that this is preventable. The students have been able to help with that. They've been a part of it and helped with the teaching as well.

Could UM be more helpful with these and other community efforts?

Yes and yes and yes. Then again, for them it's a matter of building a university, which is young compared to most universities. They have so much to do and so many buildings to be built, so they're trying to build their own structure.

Of course, I'm selfish, I guess, when I think about our [Gibson] school. We're only about two and a half miles at best from the university. With the proximity, you would think that they'd want to help make it safe. It would have been a nice thing for them to say to us, "Let us help you build that school. Our teachers, our education students could come out there and do their practice teaching."

There's been some talk about that, about using our school as a place for teacher training. It's so early in the game that we haven't built a structure. I'm hoping that we can build a structure where they can send their education majors out here, just like the nursing students, to do internships and that sort of thing.

How do you feel about the student architects' drawing for the Gibson School?

I thought the designs were beautiful. It just was not something that we could use because we did not have the money. I thought they were very nice and if we had money, we probably would have used one of them to build the school.

Do you feel that the work that the university has done with the community has had any influence on the university?

I think people look at the university a little bit differently. I think that more and more students are beginning to want to go to the university because they see it as the university in their back yard. It's somewhere that they could go and get the kind of education they want. I was surprised when my grandson said to me that he wanted to go to the university's law school. He'd come back from the University of Illinois and finished doing law there and just said, "I want to go to the University of Miami." He went there and he graduated two years ago. More and more young people are beginning to see that they could stay home and get the kind of education that they want right here without having to go elsewhere.

Have you seen any changes in attitude at the university because of its relationship with the community?

That's hard to say because as a trustee you don't really get involved in the academics. I'm not sure. I really can't say from where I sit what influence it has had, except for the fact that I know that more and more people are beginning to feel better about it. When people in the community see these University of Miami students coming into their homes, they know that the university is involved in the community. I think they appreciate that. As a community, we appreciate the university. Now whether they appreciate us – that's another story. Dr. [Donna] Shalala is anxious to be a part of the community and have the community more involved. Then again, because she is so new, her focus is to raise the momentum and raise a billion dollars. I think if she could do that, then she may be able to move forward and see how she may be able to

help more in the community. She's been very visible and [has] come into the community to let the people know that she is here and that she supports them. She's been good for the university. She's put them on the map. She's put them in the newspaper, getting more and more universal attention.

The Cityzens Project

Hector Burga
Matthew Lister
Natalia Miyar
University of Miami School of Architecture

Cityzens, a project begun by students of the University of Miami School of Architecture, employs the process of architectural design as a tool for community enhancement. Influenced by the architecture school's philosophy that the built environment plays a vital role in promoting a sense of community, these students designed a program to encourage individual participation in community action.

After a year of preparation, which included fundraising, recruitment and the development of an innovative curriculum, the project began with an intensive summer program open to students from the three high schools local to the West Coconut Grove Community: Coral Gables High School, Ransom Everglades High School and Carrollton High School. Half the students participating were residents of West Coconut Grove.

What followed were three intensive weeks in which the students were exposed to the fundamental principles of architecture and urban design, while learning basic skills in drawing, composition and computer graphics. Besides providing an architectural foundation, emphasis was also given to workshops that explored issues of consensus, team-building and self-awareness. These tools were then used to develop youth-driven community enhancement projects for the West Grove to be implemented in an after-school program during the subsequent year.

ACTION COMBATS APATHY:
THE SIX COMPONENTS OF THE CITYZENS PROJECT

Who Are You? The Cityzens Project started by asking a simple question

Photo: University of Miami photography students

Photomontage (left/right) by D. Davis & Alexis Garcia

of all participants: Who are you? This question threaded its way through all of the work carried out in the three weeks. It was a point of departure for the students, a foundation from which they began to explore their identity as it relates to architecture. As the three weeks continued, the question was revisited several times in the context of site visits, slide shows and discussions. Ultimately, the aim was to find new answers by exploring the built environment.

The Vanguard Expedition: On the opening day of the program, the Cityzens embarked on their first mission, "The Vanguard Expedition." Equipped with a map of the community, the Cityzens first used instant photography to document specific architectural elements of the place. As they moved through the community, the route was marked on the map recording the time of arrival and personal impressions provoked by each element. This method of documentation allowed the map to be transformed into a telling narrative describing both the built environment and each Cityzen's relationship to this environment. After a first day filled with first impressions, the map continued to be used as an ongoing collage of the Cityzen's experience in West Coconut Grove.

Collecting Urban Evidence and the Urban Diary: After the Vanguard expedition, the Cityzens returned to West Coconut Grove and began to develop a more intimate understanding of the elements that compose the urban environment. Referring to these elements as "Urban Evidence," the Cityzens looked at the buildings of the place and also recorded and collected artifacts, including plant life, signage, furniture and color. As the students had no formal training in drawing they were encouraged to use collage techniques in order to document Urban

Evidence in an efficient and effective manner. The documentation was carried out using the "Urban Diary," the Cityzens' version of the architectural sketchbook. This tool allowed the Cityzens to collect pieces of information, or evidence, which would later be used for the composition of a photomontage.

Photomontage: After the collection of urban evidence, the Cityzens were divided in teams and assigned subjects reflecting the major urban themes found in the community. The task was not only to design a well-composed photomontage but also to recreate a narrative from the pieces they had collected, a narrative that would be their own reinterpretation of the place. The photographs, drawings of buildings and artifacts became creative pieces that were both analyses of the local architecture and rich portraits of the community.

Pathways for Implementation: The final week of the summer program was dedicated to its most exciting component. The Cityzens, equipped with an understanding of the architectural and cultural assets of the community, began to explore the ways in which they could use the design tools they had learned to develop enhancement projects for the neighborhood. For three days, the Cityzens brainstormed and worked together to come up with "The Coconut Strut." Recognizing the importance of focusing on achievable goals, The Coconut Strut was conceived as a targeted cleanup and enhancement of specific routes in the community. The process begins with a Cityzens' sponsored town meeting where the Cityzens work with the community to determine the route for the Coconut Strut. After the route is determined the Cityzens design and implement projects along the route that make the Coconut Strut a safe

Photomontage by Alison Wiley & Brian Laing

and pleasurable walking experience through the community. These projects include a route cleanup, creative uses of empty lots, building repair and enhancement, landscaping and Coconut Strut identifying signage.

Empowerment: Fundamentally, the Cityzens after-school program will be an ongoing community-driven, participatory process that fosters civic responsibility and rebuilds civic life. The Cityzens project strives to offer students the chance to develop their own tools of empowerment through an understanding of their built environment.

We hope that through this exchange of knowledge and resources, individuals from the university and the Coconut Grove community will gain a forum of discussion; a place where the gap between the theory and practice of architecture can be breached.

Youth Social Action and Positive Development in West Coconut Grove

Etiony Aldarando, Ph.D.
University of Miami School of Education
Department of Educational and Psychological Studies

Lisa Martinez
Senior Advisor on Education Policy and Youth Initiatives to
Mayor Manuel Diaz, City of Miami

INTRODUCTION

Over the past decade or so a cacophony of voices have raised concerns about problems experienced by youth and about our collective responsibility as parents, teachers, health officials, community activists, faith leaders, policy makers, business owners, and professionals to address these problems and promote healthy youth development. Parents concerned about safety issues are increasingly vigilant and proactive in protecting their children from such threats as violence and drug use now webbed into the fabric of our social life. Teachers concerned about school failure and the strengthening of academic standards are working harder than ever to provide young people with the academic skills and knowledge needed to succeed in an increasingly technological world. Public health officials concerned with high rates of health problems (e.g., HIV infection, AIDS, diabetes, asthma) and problem behaviors (e.g., cigarette smoking, drug use, unprotected sex) among youth—particularly in predominantly African-American and Latino communities—are targeting prevention efforts towards young people. Policy makers attentive to the projected strength of our economy in an increasingly global and ethnically diverse business environment are worried about young people's readiness to join the work force and are looking for ways to help them become "productive adults". To this partial list we could add the yearn for a richer moral and spiritual life often voiced by faith leaders, community activists, and other youth advocates attentive to the inner lives of young people.

The collective wisdom and commitment of this choir has important implications for the long-term viability and efficacy of the work being done by the Initiative for Urban and Social Ecology in the community of West Coconut Grove described in this volume. Like other poor inner-city neighborhoods of color around the country, a high proportion of youth from West Coconut Grove drop out without completing high school (between 26% and 50%) and are known to engage in high risk behaviors such unprotected sex and drug use. As a result the rates of drug addiction, sexually transmitted diseases, HIV and AIDS are alarmingly high among this group of youngsters. With a median family household income of less than $15,000 most young people in this community live in poverty.

A healthy and prosperous West Coconut Grove of the sort "imagined"

by the members of INUSE must reduce risks, foster positive youth development, and promote the transformation of unsafe and unjust social conditions. A healthy and prosperous West Coconut Grove must take care of its young people and equip them with the skills, knowledge, and resources to achieve well-ness for themselves, those around them, and the community at large. The purpose of this chapter is to describe the role that community programs for youth development and social action youth initiatives can play in promoting positive youth development and social transformation in West Coconut Grove. The chapter is based on three basic assumptions: (a) that the future well being of West Coconut Grove rests, in part, on raising generations of healthy, skilled, competent, responsible, and socio-politically matured citizens, (b) that community life in the West Coconut Grove can be transformed to promote healthy lives and social justice, and (c) that young people can contribute to the creation of healthier and more just ways of living in West Coconut Grove. Accordingly, the chapter describes the nature of community youth development and social actions programs and offers a sketch of a positive youth development and social action initiative being developed at the Virrick Park Community Center in the West Grove.

COMMUNITY YOUTH PROGRAMS

There is a wide range of community youth programs designed to improve the quality of life for young people (i.e., after school care programs, community schools, drug prevention programs, sex education programs, mentoring programs, et cetera). Although there is considerable variability among programs in their specific goals and design characteristics, experts in the field suggest that youth programs can be characterized as "prevention/problem-centered" programs or as "positive youth development" programs (Eccles & Gootman, 2002). The first type of program focuses on specific problems and risks (e.g., drug-abuse, teen pregnancy, school violence, HIV infection, cigarette smoking, juvenile delinquency) faced by youth. Positive youth development programs tend to emphasize the acquisition and development of

104

"assets" (e.g., good health habits, emotional self-regulation skills, connectedness with peers and adults, commitment to civic engagement) thought to facilitate positive youth development rather than strategies for dealing with specific problems (Lerner & Benson, 2003). However, differences between prevention and positive development programs are often blurred in practice. There is increased support for the idea that programs designed to promote positive youth development and to prevent specific problems from occurring have the greatest potential to improve the life of youth (e.g., Bumbarger & Greenberg, 2002). A recent review of experimental and quasi-experimental evaluations of

Table 1: Assets for the Promotion of Positive Youth Development*

PHYSICAL DEVELOPMENT	INTELLECTUAL DEVELOPMENT
Good Health Habits	Essential life Skills
Good Health Risk Management Skills	Vocational Skills
	School Success
	Multicultural Knowledge

*Adapted from Eccles & Gootman, 2002 and Catalano, et al., 2002.

community programs for youth conducted by the national Committee on Community-Level Programs for Youth (CCLPY) (Eccles & Gootman, 2002, p. 194) revealed that participation in CYPs "is associated with increases in such outcomes as motivation, academic performance, self-esteem, problem-solving abilities, positive health decisions, interpersonal skills, and parent-child relations, as well as decreases in alcohol and tobacco use, depressive symptoms, weapon carrying, and violent behavior".

What makes for a good community youth program? What makes them effective? To date, no clear consensus has emerged about the unique features and objectives of programs associated with positive outcomes. Table 1 lists various assets considered important for the promotion of positive development in youth. With respect to the relative value of specific assets, it is better to have more assets than having few, however, access to the full range of assets is not as important as having a combination of assets across domains. Young people are better prepared to deal with the multiple challenges of life and successfully transition into adulthood when they can draw from a combination of physical, intellectual, psychological, and social resources to do so.

To be sure, the above-mentioned assets do not develop in a relational vacuum. The effectiveness of any community youth program rests not only in the richness of the activities and experiences provided to the youth but also in the quality of the relational context in which these experiences take place. CYPs must take place in settings where young people are respected, honored, welcomed, and protected if they are to become involved and thrive. Moreover, experts in the field suggest that youth programs should at the very least aim to provide young people with:

• Safe facilities and practices that increase collaboration and decrease confrontational peer interactions;
• Clear and consistent age appropriate rules and expectations;
• Continuity of activities and age appropriate monitoring;
• Warm, responsive, supportive and direct communication;
• Opportunities for meaningful inclusion regardless of race, gender, ethnicity, sexual orientation, and physical ability;
• Opportunities to participate and reinforce socially appropriate behaviors and expectations;
• Opportunities for youth-based practices that support autonomy, personal responsibility, and community engagement;
• Opportunities to learn physical, psychological, intellectual, and social skills;
• A forum for the coordination and synergy among family, school, and community efforts (Eccles & Gootman, 2002).

SOCIAL JUSTICE AND SOCIAL ACTION YOUTH INITIATIVES

Community Youth Programs of the sort described in the preceding sec-

PSYCHOLOGICAL DEVELOPMENT	SOCIAL DEVELOPMENT
Positive Self-Regard	Connectedness to Parents, Peers, and Other Adults
Good Conflict Resolution Skills	Commitment to Civic Engagement
Pro-Social Values	Sense of Place and Integration in Larger Social Network
Strong Moral Character	Attachement to Prosocial / Conventional Institutions such as School, and Church
Good Coping Skills	Ability to Function in Diverse Cultural Contexts
Spirituality or Sense of a "Larger Purpose"	
Optimism and Belief in the Future	
Clear and Positive Personal and Social Identity	
Autonomy, Responsibility for Self and Self-determination	
Self-Efficacy	
Mastery Motivation and Positive Achievement Motivation	

tion are designed to equip young people to face the challenges of grow-ing up in a complex society and to ease their transition into adulthood. Additionally, many of these programs see the production of healthy individuals as a precursor of healthier communities. These are without doubt laudable aims. However, a growing number of scholars and com-munity organizers now maintain that the realization of these goals is insufficient to sustain the long-term well being of young people and their communities (e.g., Evans & Prilleltensky, 2004; Lerner & Benson, 2003). More often than not, successful CYPs guide youth safely into adulthood without there being noticeable intentional changes in the conditions that interfere with their positive development in the first place. Proponents of social action initiatives with youth increasingly argue that the promotion of social justice and the development of social change and social action skills are essential to the development of healthy individuals and communities in a democratic society (e.g., Ginwright & James, 2002; Lerner, 2004; Ungar, 2004). In addition to assets related to personal well-being a social justice orientation to youth development promotes the attainment of critical knowledge, ana-lytic skills, and leadership capacity (i.e., organizational, planning, consensus building, and execution skills) needed for young people to

Table 2: Principles, Practices, and Outcomes of Social Justice Oriented Youth Development Programs

PRINCIPLES	PRACTICES	OUTCOMES
Analyzes Power in Social Relationships	Political education; learning about social change strategizing; reflecting about the use and misuse of power in one's own life	Ability to define problems; critical thinking; socio-political awareness
Makes Identity Central	Joining groups and organizations that support identity development; reading and discussing identity affirming mate-rials; evaluating the presence and role of stereotypes regarding one's identity	Development of pride regarding one's identity; awareness of how socio-political forces influence identity; feel-ing of being part of something meaningful and productive; capacity to build solidarity with others with like concerns and interests
Promotes Systemic Social Change	Working to end social inequality; refraining form activites and behaviors that are oppressive to others	Sense of life purpose; greater empathy for the suffering of others; heightened sense of optimism
Encourage Collective Action	Getting involved in collective efforts to challenge and improve local and national sytems and institutions; com-munity organizing; creating forums for the expression and dissemination of youth perspective	Capacity to change personal, relation-al, and community conditions; empowerment and positive orientation toward life circumstances

be meaningful contributors to the transformation and healthy development of their communities (Ginwright & James, 2002). As Evans and Prilleltensky (in press, p.18) argue, we should aim to "support young people in building capacities and to create opportunities for youth to work alongside with adults to address harmful conditions. We foster resilience and promote human and community development by equipping youth with skills and by providing them with opportunities to use them in ways to challenge inequality. This is a dynamic, experiential, and self-reinforcing process. Youth gain skills, a sense of belonging, and a deeper understanding of themselves and the world through social action. Youth are more inclined to act as they develop skills, interpersonal competencies, and socio-political awareness."

Although the aims of youth social action initiatives vary according to the lived experiences of young people in different communities, in practice the process by which these initiatives develop is one in which young people work together to 1. define problems affecting their individual, family, or community life, 2. investigate the causes of the problem, 3. generate possible solutions or strategies to deal with the problems, 4. gather and organize resources (both human and material resources) to support the implementation of the chosen strategy, 5. implement the strategy, and 6. evaluate the effectiveness of the intervention (see Lewis, 1998). This is a youth led process, often facilitated by adult members of the community (e.g., parents, teachers, church members, et cetera). Table 2 shows a related set of principles, practices, and outcomes of social justice oriented youth development programs based on the work by Ginwright and James (2002).

Virrick Park Positive Leaders and Social Action Program (PLSAP)
Over the past three years the City of Miami has been promoting the development of Virrick Park Community Center (VPCC) as a catalyst for community engagement and development in West Coconut Grove. The mission of the VPCC is to expose the community to opportunities in education, athletics, arts, and ways to reinvest in one's own community through innovative programming. The Community Center is run by the City of Miami and has a community based committee officially approved by the City to oversee the activities and programs. The center has various programs in place to respond to the needs of different age cohorts in the community including a seniors walking club, seniors fitness classes and movie days, a men's "black top" basketball league, a

junior black top basketball league, after school care for children, and a summer camp.

The Positive Leaders and Social Action Program (PLSAP) is the latest community initiative undertaken at VCC. The program is the outgrowth of a grassroots initiative spearheaded by then Coconut Grove Elementary school teacher, Lisa Martinez, and City of Miami Police Officer, Maurice Austin who were concerned about the unmet educational, personal, and social needs of Coconut Grove residents, in particular children. Three years ago, they devised a model of community engagement and youth positive development centered on cross-generational mentoring and leadership training and embedded in a network of supportive community resources such as schools, parks, businesses, government agencies, and local community based organizations interested in the well being of children in West Coconut Grove. With the financial support provided by professional basketball player and former Miami Heat star Brian Grant, Ms. Martinez and Officer Austin formed a non-profit organization, Positive Partnership, Inc., to carry on their initiative.

As part of the Positive Partners initiative each child was matched with a community mentor with whom they kept in regular contact via email and interacted in series of planned activities (e.g., careers day, field trips) designed for the young boys and girls in the program to receive adult guidance and support as the children broadened their view of the world and their place in it. The youth also attended weekly meetings led by Officer Austin and Ms. Martinez, which focused on conflict resolution, problem solving, and self-regulation skills. These meetings also aimed to increase the youth's awareness of community issues and to explore community service as a viable way for students to give back to their community. Over the past two years their Positive Partners Mentorship Model has been conducted in collaboration with Coconut Grove Elementary, F.S. Tucker Elementary School, and the Gibson Charter School. Anecdotal data based on reports for participants and their parents suggested that youth of the Positive Partnerships Program has made important contributions to the life of the children in the program.

In a relatively short period of time the program model has gained considerable local and municipal support. Mayor Manuel Diaz, Virrick

Park's facility manager, Wesley Carroll, the City of Miami Parks and Recreation Department, the South West Coconut Grove NET office, and the Coconut Grove Chamber of Commerce have strongly supported the Positive Partnerships Mentorship Program. This support ranged from providing a location for events and meetings, transportation, introduction to local organizations, and a venue for communication with the community. Inspired, in part, by the vision and success of the Positive Partnership Mentoring Program, last year Ms. Martinez was asked to serve as Senior Advisor on Education Policy and Youth Initiatives to Mayor Manuel Diaz and to spearhead the Mayor's

Mentoring Initiative in the City's schools.

After a vigorous process of growth and experimentation the Positive Partnership Mentorship Program is now at point of expansion, systematization, and evaluation, which we hope would make it possible for the program to be used by other communities through the city. The Positive Partnerships Program, Inc. has committed to fund the development and piloting of the program for the next two years. In collaboration with counseling psychology faculty and students from the University of Miami we are now refining the community service compo-

Figure 1: Major Components of Virrick Park Youth Positive Leaders and Social Action Program

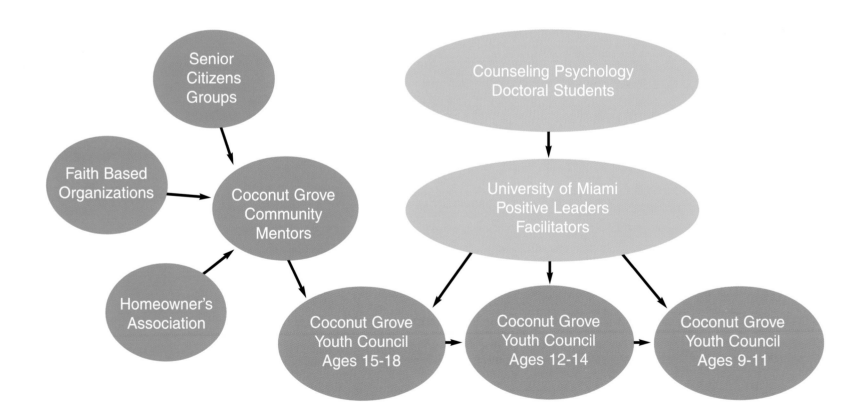

Photos: Etiony Aldarando

nent of the program and making community engagement and social action core dimensions. We are also laying the foundation for the development of training and research components that would prepare University of Miami students develop knowledge and skills in community organizing, social action, and applied social science research methods.

The newly named Positive Leaders and Social Action Program aims to help young men and women from the West Grove develop personal assets, leadership capacity, and socio-political awareness through involvement in social action and mentoring initiatives. Figure 1 shows the major components of this program and their relationship with each other.

The PLSAP is designed to promote civic engagement and social action among three core youth groups —one for young boys and girls in 4th, 5th and 6th grades, one for middle school age kids, and one for high school teens. With the assistance of University of Miami Positive Leaders Facilitators and Grove Community Mentors youth in each group will participate in age appropriate activities designed to help them develop competencies in skills such as communication, non-violent problem resolution, public speaking, group processes, consensus building, development of social change strategies, and execution and coordination of social action initiatives. The participation of all groups in the process of civic engagement and social change is meant to generate an institutional culture that values, supports, and models commitment justice and the improvement of civic society. This culture is also promoted through both the youth and adult mentoring compo-

nents of the program. As part of the program youth are involved in a multileveled mentoring system where young boys and girls not only receive mentoring from UM facilitators and community mentors but also have the opportunity to serve as mentors to younger members of the program. Thus, youth council members are both mentored by adult members of the community and are also mentors to the junior council members. In turn, junior council members serve as mentors to the younger cohort of positive leaders. The specific focus of the mentoring process will vary according to the individual needs of the children involved, the assigned group activities, and the interpersonal group dynamics.

Although the Positive Leaders and Social Action Program is open to all interested participants, the first phase of recruitment has focused on students participating in the after school program and in the Junior Black Top Basketball League. The aim for this pilot year is to recruit 24 to 30 young boys and girls across age groups. We are also in the process of identifying appropriate community mentors. These community mentors are being recruited from the community's homeowner's association, senior citizens' groups, and local churches (with the help of the Mayor's Faith Based Initiative). Community mentors will sign up as City volunteers. They will commit to seeing their mentee's at least once a month during program activities and communicating via email on a weekly basis.

Positive Leaders Facilitators will include volunteers from the University of Miami Golden Drum Scholarship Program and the Counseling Psychology Program. Golden Drum Scholars are Florida high school graduates of African-American or Black Caribbean descent recognized for their high levels of academic achievement and commitment to community service. These students will work under the supervision of counseling psychology doctoral students with training in developmental psychology, conflict resolution, supportive interventions for children, and social action strategies.

The Positive Leaders Facilitators and their supervisors have a very important role in the development and implementation of the Positive Leaders and Social Action Program. They will be responsible for helping coordinate age appropriate activities; facilitate Coconut Grove Youth Council, Junior Council, and Future Positive Leaders meetings; developing a regular form of communication with all mentors (via email); communicating with mentee's families on a regular basis via phone calls and written communication to assure that there is a clear understanding of student needs; documenting attendance; overseeing mentoring across age cohort; and coordinating efforts and facilitating Coconut Grove Youth Council/Junior Council Projects.

CONCLUDING REMARKS

Youth across the nation are facing very serious challenges to their quality of life and their ability to become productive and involved adult citizens and leaders. This is also true for the youth of West Coconut Grove. There is no clear solution, no single policy change, no one program, no one social experiment that would clear the way for young boys and girls to live safe, healthy lives, with dignity and sense of purpose. And, as it should be clear from the work of my colleagues in this book as well as the writing of many others in our respective fields, it is not news to suggest that the solutions, whatever they may be, require greater integration of community, professional, business, university, and government resources within a reasoned network of interventions than it is now the case. We argue in this chapter that the solutions must also include the input of youth in the promotion of wellness and social justice in their communities. We are aware, as the result of the last presidential elections so poignantly remind us, that it is very difficult to promote change that runs counter to the prevailing ethos of a society with social structures and institutions entrenched in gender and racial inequalities, uneven distribution of wealth, social isolation and dislocation, and the instrumental use of aggression in the pursuit of self and national interests. Against the odds, thus, we believe the Positive Leaders and Social Action Program outlined in this chapter to be a small step in the right direction.

REFERENCES

Catalano, R. F., Berglund, M. L., Ryan, J. A. M., Lonczak, H. S., & Hawkins, J. D. (2002). Positive youth development in the United States: Research findings on evaluations of positive youth development programs. Prevention and Treatment, 5, NP.

Eccles, J. S., Gootman, J. A., (2002). Community programs to promote youth development. Washington, DC: National Academy Press.
Evans, S. D. & Prilleltensky, I. (in press). Youth Civic Engagement: Promise and Peril.

Ginwright, S., & James, T. (2002). From assets to agents of change: Social justice, organizing and youth development. New Directions for Youth Development, 96, 27-46.

Lerner, R. (2004). Liberty: Thriving and civic engagement among America's youth. London: Sage.

Lerner, R. M., & Benson, P. L. (2003). Developmental assets and asset-building communities : implications for research, policy, and practice. New York: Kluwer Academic/Plenum Publishers.

Lewis, B. A. (1998). The kid's guide to social action. Minneapolis, MN: Free Spirit Publishing.

Lewis-Charp, H., Cao Yu, H., Soukamneuth, S., & Lacoe, J. (2003). Extending the Reach of Youth Development Through Civic Activism: Outcomes of the Youth Leadership for Development Initiative: Social Policy Research Associates.

Morsillo, J. (2003). Social Action with Youth: A beginning to empowerment and well-being. In E. Martin & J. Booth (Eds.), Courageous Research (pp. 99-114). Melbourne: Common Ground Publishing and Victoria University.

Morsillo, J., & Prilleltensky, I. (in press). Social action with youth: Interventions,Evaluation, and psychopolitical validity. Journal of Community Psychology.

Ungar, M. (2004). Nurturing hidden resilience in troubled youth. Toronto, University of Toronto Press.

A Community Organizer Speaks

Daniella Levine
Human Services Coalition

COMMUNITY BUILDING PLUS CIVIC ENGAGEMENT
EQUALS SOCIAL CHANGE

The Initiative for Urban and Social Ecology (INUSE) has conducted its work in partnership with area nonprofits, political leaders and community activists. The project is ambitious and visionary. But it has been conducted, of necessity, in the absence of a community-wide plan and without the participation of a sustained leadership. As a university sponsored effort, its primary purpose was teaching and scholarship, not community-building. Without a cohesive, community voice or organization to promote the community's interests, the effort could not be sustained. In essence, the Center created a sense of hope in the absence of a community infrastructure to sustain that hope. The dilemma for this effort and any community building effort in Miami Dade today is how to jumpstart positive social change when our neighborhoods and region have suffered from lack of investment, social capital and leadership. Civic engagement—supported by investment in community institutions that can foster civic engagement—is, I believe, the missing ingredient for creating long-term community change.

While the West Grove efforts were underway, a parallel path led me to seek other ways to secure social and economic justice for all county residents. I founded the Human Services Coalition (HSC) in 1996 in conjunction with other community leaders to address unequal access to health care, income, education, housing and other opportunities: in other words, to increase access to prosperity. HSC developed civic engagement and leadership development strategies that would inspire those who lacked access, and the institutions that serve them, to play a more active role in the shaping of the policies that affect their lives. The HSC model is based on the idea that active participation in local community building efforts is essential for the development of civic engagement and leadership skills that can then be transferred for use in the public policy arena. Furthermore, specific technical assistance provided to those engaged in community building can lead to the creation of civic infrastructure, vital for the sustainability of the efforts.

But what we have learned through our efforts is that this kind of major community change is best achieved through a hybrid approach that activates different scales of action. Neighborhood building combined with countywide support for leadership development and public policy

Photo: Richard Shepard

focused civic engagement will fuel a sense of hope. Community engagement in targeted areas will thus stimulate broader senses of duty in terms of the city, the state and, eventually, the nation. In time, a multi-scalar commitment to collective development can reverse the social capital deficit that has eroded trust in our civic structures.

Hope is created when the access to opportunity is made tangible. When community stakeholders sense these opportunities for a better life and pursue them, not only will individuals and families prosper, but also our communities will continue to cohere. This will constitute a win-win-win for our communities. More opportunities lead to more prosperity; more prosperity, more unity; more unity, more hope—a positive, reinforcing circle that will counteract the growing frustration, poverty and disenfranchisement now being perpetuated in too many of our communities. The trend towards balkanization and walled communities will be reversed as diverse communities come to understand their mutual self interest and shared destinies in a dynamic, evolving global gateway city and region.

DEFINING COMMUNITY: WHAT IS THE PURPOSE?

People live in neighborhoods on the basis of tradition, history, convenience, and cost. When neighborhoods are viewed as deficient due to high rates of crime, lack of code enforcement, high levels of absentee landlords, or social indicators such as poverty, substance abuse and child abuse, then government and the human service sector may intervene to shore up the neighborhood's coping mechanisms.

However, these interventions are seldom planned or coordinated. Residents may need to become full-time consumers of such services to obtain needed support. State agencies demand multiple visits and interrogation to provide economic assistance. Social agencies may have wait lists or other barriers to care. Health providers may charge fees that limit effective access. Faith institutions may provide charity through food or clothing distribution, on an emergency basis. Sustained, orchestrated help is hard to find. All of these inefficient and inhumane processes serve the institutions, but do not adequately serve the people or the communities.

The people who live in these communities often become so consumed with the details of daily coping that they may lose touch with their sense of place and personal power. These residents typically have little sense of control over their own lives, and certainly do not have confidence in their ability to improve their communities. Community-building institutions, community centers or social action agencies are too often designed by and for the professional staff, and do not include a focus on sustained engagement and empowerment of residents they seek to help.

Miami is well known for this lack of "social capital" and its inability to hold elected, government and agency officials accountable for their actions and spending. The net result of this lack of investment in people participation is that we have too many disenfranchised people whose active participation in rebuilding troubled communities is vitally needed but untapped. At the root of this lack of community building is lack of trust in our system of government and structure of our society.

113

Lack of participation only serves to perpetuate low civic investment and trust. How can we break this cycle of self-perpetuating low social capital cycle? I was determined to find out and press to change this negative local paradigm.

I founded the Human Services Commission (HSC) in 1995 as an outgrowth of my work with the League of Women Voters of Dade County, and my social justice work at Legal Services of Greater Miami, the Guardian Ad Litem program and elsewhere. I had joined the League within my first month of residence in Miami Dade, arriving in 1983 while still finishing my law and social work degrees. I was attracted to the League because of its dedication to promoting civic engagement. I was focused on participation in the design of effective social programs—the areas I was devoted to since age 13, when I first volunteered as an after school tutor. HSC became the vehicle for combining these concerns.

CIVIC ENGAGEMENT AT THE CORE OF COMMUNITY BUILDING

In 1998, The National Commission on Civic Renewal observed an alarming increase in passivity and disengagement among citizens of all types and an absence of confidence in the individual's ability to effect change. In a time that cries out for civic action, we are in danger of becoming a nation of spectators . These trends threaten to undermine the participatory values on which our democracy is based.

Our democracy was designed as a "deferential-participant" model to assure that the many will defer to those few believed to have superior judgment. However, to counter the elitist tendencies of this model that potentially relegates most Americans to second class status with no access to power or public decision-making, our democracy requires public participation to assure checks and balances upon the power of the few. Throughout our history, thanks to our strong spirits and the power of collective action, Americans have created countless ways to assert their desire for more direct participation. In 1831, Alexis de Tocqueville was able to report that Americans were a nation of "joiners", who actively shaped their society through civic, social and political affiliations.

Today, 250 years after our nation's birth, Americans are volunteering in

record numbers to help those less fortunate or build strong communities, but the majority of us are not participating in democracy. Voter registration and voting are down to historic lows, despite resurgence in the recent heavily publicized national elections. Public attitudes toward government suggest the highest levels of distrust and dismay. The party system still dominates political outcomes, but participation in the party structure is dwindling.

Nothing less than the future and vitality of our democracy is at stake, with the tyranny of the few already resulting in decision-making that benefits the few over the many.

Rekindling the flames of participatory democracy is incumbent on each and every citizen. As individuals and communities, we must create the mechanisms to reclaim each person's power to contribute to the betterment of society. We must find ways to develop healthy civic habits throughout every aspect of our lives, starting with our young people, or we will wake up one day and find we are too late.

The Community Prosperity Initiative (CPI), a countywide collaborative effort, is a vehicle for broad civic engagement. It was created by HSC in 2003 with the intention of revitalizing passion for our democracy, at every stage and in every community, from birth to grave.

BUILDING A COMMUNITY AND ECONOMY THAT WORK FOR ALL

"To get to common ground, we must go to higher ground." These words, written by Reverend Jim Wallis, Founder of Sojourners magazine and author of numerous books on the subject of how we treat our fellow human beings, now guides my work. Democracy must be protected so that we can have the kind of country that reflects the highest levels of humanity: mutual respect, tolerance, free exchange of ideas, and opportunities to pursue happiness. People are taking our democracy for granted, and what the majority of caring and honorable people want is not reflected in our social policy. These people, that is to say most of us, are not participating in all sorts of ways needed to assure the greatest good for the greatest number of people.

Human Services Coalition grew out of a desire to create a place that could focus on rebuilding social capital to fight against the tyranny of the few. If we connect all who care about such education and engagement programs in a comprehensive way, our joint efforts will permeate society and tip the tide towards broad participation.

HSC has capitalized on its reputation for telling the truth, for bringing diverse people together and for getting things done to battle the poverty that erodes social capital and discourages participation. In the fall of 2002, the 2000 Census identified the City of Miami as the poorest large city in the country. [...] With leadership from the Mayors of the City and County and the Greater Miami Chamber of Commerce, HSC declared a new war on poverty called the "Greater Miami Prosperity Campaign"; its goal was to lift low-wage workers out of poverty. The Campaign focuses on increasing residents' use of the federal Earned Income Tax Credit and other economic benefits. An initial investment from the John S. and James L. Knight Foundation yielded a thousand-fold return on investment, with $63 million new dollars entering the ... The Campaign has now been replicated in several counties around the state, and the Florida Prosperity Campaign will be launched in 2005.

Following the advice of Reverend Wallis, HSC next sought "higher ground" by launching a Community Prosperity Initiative (CPI) not only to expand our prior efforts but also to address the underlying causes of our ranking and seek to reverse the trends. CPI's mission is to move Miami-Dade from among the poorest counties to #1 in community prosperity, by engaging persons from six key sectors (community, business, government, academia, philanthropy, and media) who are both willing to commit to the effort and believe that the mission can be achieved.

Specifically, the Initiative will raise awareness, share knowledge, gain involvement and provide a blueprint for social change by accomplishing five broad goals:

• To build public understanding about the need and opportunity for change;

• To define measures for success;

• To develop inventory of community strengths and assets that will support the initiative;

• To support cross-sector work groups to define, conduct, connect and monitor plans for change; and

• To build countywide, cross-sector leadership and sustainability for change.

Impacts will be measured across three vectors: financial (related to income and access to good jobs); unity (incorporating people's sense of engagement); and hope (incorporating a sense of opportunity).

Organization and leadership are the keys to tackle this ambitious agenda effectively. We therefore created a cross sector Leadership Council to guide the Initiative, and a Global Council of Advisors to inform participants about changes, opportunities, best practice, innovative models, funding strategies and contacts in the wider environment that can help us achieve our goals. To ensure that there are knowledgeable persons who can fuel these efforts, we will foster leadership development for those who can help us articulate the vision, share the message, raise consciousness and foster teamwork within and across sectors. We will particularly seek youth leadership, to assure the sustainability of the effort over time.

The Initiative draws upon baseline demographic data on our County prepared by the Brookings Institution that revealed the growing income gaps and conditions that inhibit the growth and vitality of our middle class. Additional data relevant to our effort will be analyzed to inform our work. Education, housing, asset development, income level and transportation are all at the heart of these findings. We are also planning to conduct a countywide values inventory (what do we stand for, what do our residents think we should stand for) using state of the art instruments developed by Corporate Tools . The Initiative will link efforts to those of others with others already working towards a common vision of community prosperity, by sharing these findings and analysis at a series of inclusive community forums and dialogues.

Dialogue will lead to goal identification and action. To measure the progress we are making, we will set benchmarks across indicators: Is more affordable housing available? Are more of our residents being educated and prepared for sustainable jobs? Do the salaries of the jobs in our local economy provide a self-sufficiency wage? Is the level of savings and home ownership increasing? Are we better reflecting the values that our residents believe are needed to build the community we seek?

Each sector will participate in the dialogue and contribute uniquely. Academia will help us develop benchmarks and measure progress and connect us to students for internships and faculty for applied research. Philanthropy will invest strategically to support our goals. Government will provide financial support to the extent possible and identify and support initiatives that remove barriers and create pathways to success. Business will promote internal and external policies that support the changes needed to achieve the vision, consistent with principles of corporate social responsibility that also reflect sound business practices. Media will help us to communicate and engage, using innovative strategies that contribute to a sense of community cohesion and hope. Community residents and organizations will seek accountability from all sectors, to assure that the effort is not detoured by special interests.

An impressive array of local, state and national leaders wrote their initial suggestions for local community-building. Many of these thoughts were incorporated into the publication: "Building Community Prosperity in Miami-Dade" (January 2004). This publication was the first effort to describe the Initiative's challenges, opportunities and strategies. It included reflections from representatives of each of the sectors who were willing to state publicly how they think we can create a community that helps us to achieve individual and shared dreams. The Initiative will need the voices of thousands of others; additional perspectives on the role of education, transportation, and housing are

especially needed.

Innovative tools for community engagement that bridge divides of income, race, class, language, lifestyle and geography are needed. The Initiative will design these so that people can participate in their own ways in their own time and space. Communications methodologies such as the use of "appreciative inquiry" will create new platforms for real dialogue and hope. Communications platforms as varied as house meetings or weblogs, and imaginative devices such as scenario planning, will assure diversity of participation. Inclusion of cultural celebration and recognition for participation will help connect through the heart and soul as well as the head...

To accomplish this bold and ambitious plan we need to be audacious. HSC has already accomplished something unprecedented in the county: engagement of the business sector in the promotion of economic benefits to the low wage workforce. To accomplish CPI's mission we need to go to a higher level of community engagement that assures cross sector understanding and caring. This requires tremendous leadership and vision.

To my amazement, not one of the many incredible human beings I approached in 2004 to serve on the "Leadership Council" has balked. All seem genuinely honored to be considered to fit the criteria for leadership: passion for the mission, hope it can be accomplished, commitment to make it happen, humility about learning from others, connection to a constituency that they can engage in the work, ability to listen and learn, results orientation.

The role of education is critical to the accomplishment of CPI's mission, as data gatherer, benchmark developer and trend analyst. The University of Miami has been an early adopter, creating a campus wide committee to examine how each school and department can contribute to building community prosperity. The first step in university involvement will be completion of an assets inventory that will describe the many forms of community engagement already underway among faculty, students and staff. The West Grove effort will be a featured element, one that reflects the kind of diversity and resiliency that is Miami Dade at its best.

Photo: Richard Shepard

Miami-Dade residents are the most diverse in the world (with more foreign born than any other city), and this has led to a sense of division and isolation. Yet, Miami-Dade's people have demonstrated extraordinary caring and compassion during tragedies such as Hurricane Andrew in 1992, and have developed tremendous capacity to relate to people regardless of race, ethnicity and income. Many of our residents have triumphed over adversity to attain success, and in so doing, have remembered their roots and how others have helped them to succeed. When we remind ourselves of this community record we are inspired to redouble our efforts. These values of understanding, compassion and giving back are at the root of everything we do.

LINKING CIVIC ENGAGEMENT STRATEGIES

HSC utilizes multiple strategies to accomplish social change including grassroots organizing, consensus building among community stakeholders, policy research and advocacy, and call to action by charismatic leadership. It is not just the variety of strategies employed that makes HSC unique, but also the manner in which HSC seeks to connect and amplify the strategies, both within the organization and through linkages among other community efforts. HSC has engaged in a variety of capacity-building efforts to assure that other groups can maximize their effectiveness with each of these strategies: incubating new organizations through fiscal sponsorship, and providing technical assistance on management functions as well as coalition-building and advocacy.

The Community Prosperity Initiative will need to create new modes of communication and bridge building that draw upon all of the social change strategies in order to achieve its audacious goals. Those engaged in grassroots organizing, for example, will need to see the benefit of engaging in consensus building with business, government and academic groups, in order to accomplish CPI's common goals. Those comfortable with policy research and advocacy will need to see the value of charismatic leadership as a vehicle for social change. Those engaged in improving their communities will need to see the connection to larger social policies, and develop the mechanisms and capacity to take part in the policy dialogue.

How will all of these strategies and efforts become empowered and aligned? Capacity building and strategic planning support will help move existing organizations to new levels of civic engagement. Training, mentoring, pairing, and joint planning all require process and content expertise. Intermediary organizations need to have the ability to sustain involvement of community residents over time. HSC has been fortunate to both receive and give such support. Unfortunately, these supports have not been adequately available in Coconut Grove during this community building initiative, leaving the activists without a sustainability strategy.

COCONUT GROVE REVISITED

INUSE developed a vision, constituents, a plan and an operation to revitalize the West Grove in a manner that would engage and empower the residents. Unfortunately, the long-term investments were not in place to assure this outcome. Market forces are pushing out long-term residents to make way for those with more money and less interest in the area's history and culture. A community infrastructure does not exist to modify and mediate these forces. The designs pioneered by UM faculty and students will now largely benefit the developers and the new residents, as older residents are priced out of the market. Other communities have been able to shape development in a way that is more inclusive of existing residents: mixed income housing, set asides for local hiring and contracting, job training and placement funds are all vehicles that assure local residents benefit economically from development.

But in the face of West Grove development, no community organization was prepared to work through a "community benefits" campaign. The values of "smart growth and sustainability" that would have led to a greater focus on the equity of the development (and thus a greater benefit to current residents) were not at the forefront of the development decisions because there was no organizational structure empowered and organized to introduce these to the decision-making process. The Center for Urban and Community Design at the University of Miami did not broaden its focus to create the sustainable structures that could engage residents to build the base of support and accountability. These structures could not have been created in the short term. A longer-term strategy to change the pattern of government and philanthropic investments, and invest in leadership building and civic engagement within the community would be needed.

The challenges of the West Grove cannot be addressed in the microcosm. It will take the whole village to support the change needed to rebuild that and our many other struggling communities. The Community Prosperity Initiative is a vehicle to galvanize such action across the county and across the sectors, demonstrating the mutual interdependence of all parts of the community and the delicate fabric that is our human capital.

I invite all stakeholders who believe in this vision of community to partner with us as we begin a strategic planning process that can change the face and the future of this County. We need local leadership, regional and global experts. It will require hope, energy, creativity, courage, grit, intelligence and most of all openness to new ideas and new voices. In short, it will require personal and communitywide commitment to change.

Are you ready?

Photo: Richard Shepard

Gregory W. Bush
University of Miami School of Arts & Sciences
Department of History

ROLE OF RELIGION

The Bahamians were those with ties in the Bahama Islands their children and their grand-children, etcetera. You will find in the churches, the Episcopal Churches and the African Orthodox Churches and even in some of the AME Churches, third, fourth, and fifth generation Bahamians, much like in Christ Church in the Grove where I grew up. When I see the children of my nieces and nephews active in the life of the church--well this is what I did, this is what my parents did. Christ Episcopal Church. and Saint Paul AMA Church have always been Bahamian and American mixed, for generations. The Bahamians always believed strongly in property ownership.
Reverend Austin Cooper

MAKING PROFESSIONAL LIFE

After I graduated from college, I came back to Miami, and I didn't want to teach, but they needed ... teachers at that time. That was 1941. My brother was still in service, my mother said that you must go and get a job because we don't have money for ... The principal called me, said I need a P.E. teacher, would you please come and work for me, so I went. I taught at Booker Washington for 3 years. I saved all the money, and I got my retirement from the state, which was 200 dollars, and told my mother I was going to Atlanta for the school of social work. There I went, and I received my master's and decided to go overseas with the American Red Cross. My mother came to me in New York, I had an aunt that lived in New York for 45 years, and this is where we spent our summers. We would go up there and stay the summer, all but my father. He never would travel with us. The only time that he came up there was the year that I graduated...because he did not want me to go overseas--with the American Red Cross. When my father said that, I think you should do such a thing, there was no recourse. Because he was the man of the house, and we obeyed him. So I

came on back to Miami. I didn't go overseas. I came and worked for the church. I [was] their secretary for a year, and then I went back into the school system. They just called, and called, "we need you." I went back to the school system. I didn't stop there. I went on to New York University, in the summer. . . I decided I wanted to take administration. I did all my work for a doctorate but writing the dissertation. The school board gave me credit, so I came back … I stayed in the system for 40 years.
Vernika Silva

Photo: Claude Etienne

IMPACT OF DE-SEGREGATION

My earliest recollections of the Grove, certainly there was segregation to be sure everywhere, but in spite of the limitations imposed from without, there was a sense of community. There was a sense of family responsibility. There was, in every neighborhood, a sense of responsibility to the family whether or not the family members were your family members by blood, or the children of neighbors.
Reverend Austin Cooper

GROWING DRUG & VIOLENCE PROBLEM

When people went out you simply left your clothes on the line and went about your business. That is no longer so, you can't do that now in Coconut Grove. For a number of reasons, the community has grown different set of values, more activities, which are not necessarily conducive to a good and wholesome community life...We also have the drug problem in the Grove. That was not so when I was a boy. Streets are not as safe as they once were. Growing up, people could, women could walk to church at night and not fear anything. Nowadays it's

somewhat risky. I don't have any fear when I go to the Grove because I grew up there, I know everybody. Still it's my home. I love it. I could never forget Coconut Grove.
Reverend Austin Cooper

ON THE GROWING USE OF ORAL HISTORY TO HELP DEFINE COMMUNITY

What became clear from my interviews and the students' work was the need to better understand the social turmoil that had beset the area by the 1960s. The fabric of urban life significantly declined as drugs, television and the suburbanization of local professionals eroded the power of role models within the community. Political palliatives did little to improve the quality of social life or the sense of political impotence felt by so many residents. Not through politics but through the church, school and social clubs one can see the power of a number of women such as Thelma Anderson Gibson in sustaining the sense of community and acting as a bridge to the larger power structure. Yet it is also clear to me that future oral history documentation should involve more interviews and sensitivity towards younger people and their problems, motivations and reactions to the conditions around them. For many reasons, the Miami area has a weak understanding of the need to build things to last- be they buildings, public spaces or communities- and lacks the sensitivity to nurture them. Oral history has the potential to help change people's attitudes and revalue the elements that make for permanence within the human experience. It can involve students at all levels as observers, or practitioners. Yet to make an impact oral history interviews need to be more widely seen by being edited and seen on local TV and heard over the radio. We need a better appreciation of the value and fascinating quality of real people in our fast paced and overly glitzy region.

Photo: Marina Mougios

Vision Plan
Architectural and Urban Design Initiatives

Richard Shepard
Eric Vogt
University of Miami School of Architecture

The University of Miami's School of Architecture has helped bring change to West Coconut Grove over a period of four years as part of a multifaceted, open-ended process of engagement. Throughout this process, the School has tried to serve as the eyes and ears and words of an evolving common will to rebuild.

The school's efforts have originated out of the Center for Urban and Community Design (CUCD). CUCD was originally established in 1992 to address the challenge of rebuilding following Hurricane Andrew, but has since broadened its focus and successfully organized a number community design projects in South Florida. At CUCD, our specific mandate has been to heighten the image and identity of places, based on an understanding of how the built environment can profoundly affect a community. Our goal has been to integrate research, teaching and service, encouraging interdisciplinary thought and action. We have also sought to bring our work to the attention of the University of Miami, local communities, and the nation.

With its commitment to neighborhood planning and contextual design, the School of Architecture is now committed to learning from West Coconut Grove residents, and assisting them to envision a brighter future. At the same time, collaborative projects by CUCD in West Coconut Grove have allowed architecture and planning students to engage in applied research and gain valuable hands-on experience. In particular, CUCD's Design/Build Studio, has offered students the chance to design affordable houses, and then see some of their designs built on vacant lots in West Coconut Grove.

CUCD has also taken a stewardship role with regard to community building efforts. Our assistance in this regard has so far included architectural, urban and landscape design projects, mapping and zoning studies, and community-efficacy assistance to help rebuild social structure.

BACKGROUND TO THE WORK

The "West Grove" is a low-income, predominantly African-American community located within minutes of the University of Miami campus. Typical of many urban neighborhoods in South Florida and across the United States, over the past 40 years crime and drug use drove many of its residents and businesses away. Within the context of Miami, the

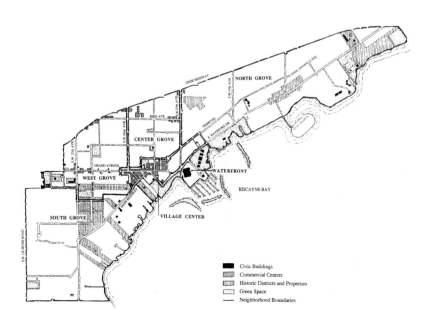

The Planning Study shows the West Grove as one of four Coconut Grove Neighborhoods.

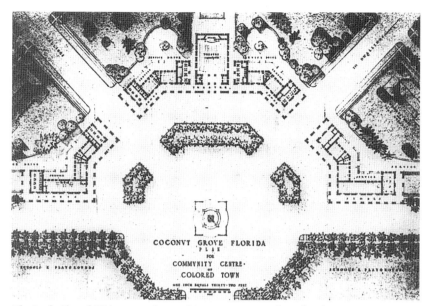

The Bright Plan of 1921 propoesed a new "Community Center for Colored Town".

Townhouse prototypes from the 1996 Coconut Grove Planning Study

neighborhood is well defined, surrounded by more affluent areas. But the legacy of neglect means that today planners and designers working there must battle misperceptions related to ethnic makeup, the stigma of past segregation policies, and community suspicion related to previous half-hearted redevelopment efforts.

Although not well attended to by planners, West Coconut Grove has not been totally ignored, however. The first study of conditions there took place in 1920. Its author, John Irwin Bright, an architect from Philadelphia, was retained by the City of Miami to study the disposition of roads and neighborhoods throughout Coconut Grove. Bright's report featured elegant drawings of proposed alterations, including a Municipal Center facing a large public park which ended at the waterfront. It also included an equally well-detailed plan for an area on the other side of the railroad tracks called "Colored Town." Colored Town was to have its own community center, encircling a large fountain, looking across a grand boulevard at schools and playgrounds.

Bright's plan must have been considered too ambitious, because the next planning work in Coconut Grove came in 1948, when a Citizens Committee for Slum Clearance was created by residents of both its East and West areas. In the years that followed, its major accomplishment was to bring sewer and water service in support of an edict outlawing backyard privies.

In 1996 the City of Miami again commissioned a team of professional planners to study Coconut Grove. Their goal was to develop a set of planning principles for improving and enhancing its variety of economic, social and physical characteristics. This study divided the area into four zones, one of which was West Coconut Grove, and today, many of the recommendations which percolated out of community meetings associated with this work are still being discussed. Among them is the desire by residents of West Coconut Grove to maintain the area's traditional Caribbean flavor and its pattern of single- and two-family homes and local shop ownership.

When the School of Architecture made its first foray into Village West, as it now likes to be called, in the fall of 2000, there was considerable concern for safety. Because the neighborhood had a reputation for drug dealing and holdups, escorts from the local Americorps chapter were enlisted as guides, and students were ferried to the area by van and moved as a huddle along its streets. But after this trip went off without incident, subsequent trips involved fewer precautions, and eventually the students became regular visitors to the neighborhood with their measuring tapes and cameras.

Early the university's engagement with the neighborhood we discovered that community-based organizations were a valuable asset in learning about the forces that united and divided it. Specifically, meetings with members of the Coconut Grove Local Development Corporation, the Homeowners and Tenants Association, and the Theodore Gibson Memorial Foundation revealed much about the area's past and its hopes for the future. Importantly, we soon found great fear of change: many residents felt it would bring new disappointments; others felt it would make their lives even more difficult; and others were suspicious that it would benefit some at the expense of others.

Community-based organizations also told us how frictions inside and-

Knight Fellows in Community Building bring their expertise to local organizations.

A Design Resource Center brings students and the community together.

outside the neighborhood had led to a poor level of success in the past in accomplishing their goals. In particular, they told of the difficulty of managing the reporting and documentation requirements for nonprofit agencies using public money. But these meetings also brought a ray of hope. Specifically, it soon became apparent that if the university were truly interested in helping over a period of years, the community could benefit tremendously from access to its nonpartisan, noncommercial expertise. For its part, the university could expect to gain valuable feedback about community-design strategies as a result of working in the area.

The presence of university students was also better received than expected. Indeed, invitations to become ever more involved in community affairs soon led us to want an in-neighborhood office. Such an office would give us more regular access to the community and provide a more continuous presence on its streets. Strangely, however, several opportunities to open such an office fell through due to fears among property owners of formalizing an agreement with the university. It was as if the idea of help was welcome, but the hand offered was not to be trusted.

Eventually, a Community Design and Resource Center was opened on Grand Avenue in a property owned by a relative newcomer to the area — a developer of affordable homes who had been a partner in past CUCD activities. This in-community center has since facilitated design presentations and community meetings and created a neutral ground for wide-ranging discussions about the future of the community.

PLANNING PRIORITIES AND COMMUNITY CONCERNS

Examples abound of educated outsiders descending on distressed neighborhoods to tell their residents how to fix their problems. Such a "parachute" approach, however, has often led to misunderstandings, and resulted in advice that is uninformed by local considerations. When CUCD begin its work in West Coconut Grove we were aware of the need to take a different approach, and we limited our early involvement to observation and asking questions. What we heard were longstanding concerns in the community: that its residents wanted to increase safety by increasing homeownership; and that they wanted to improve their main street, Grand Avenue.

Increased homeownership is widely seen as a basis for restoring stability to a community. If an area's vacant lots and abandoned buildings can be developed for new low- and moderate-income homeowners, the proportion of stakeholders increases, and community pride often returns. Families who care for the value of their homes are also more likely to show concern about aberrant street life than more transient residents or government rental-coupon holders. In West Coconut Grove, homeownership was also widely perceived as a way to provide the "connectedness" that would encourage the community to live together and prosper. Since we were in the business of educating architects, community leaders suggested that we offer a design studio to address the issue of affordable houses.

As our engagement progressed, we also realized just how united residents and business owners in Coconut Grove were in what they envisioned for their neighborhood. Families have always constituted a

The Design Resource Center looks out over Grand Avenue.

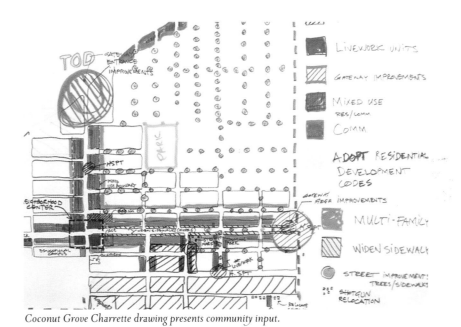

Coconut Grove Charrette drawing presents community input.

large portion of the population of Coconut Grove, and some can trace their residence there back six generations to ancestors who immigrated from Nassau or Key West to help northern whites build the first railroad and tourist hotels in South Florida. These longstanding residents wanted to see more families and family-owned businesses in their community, and they wanted their children to be able to walk safely to school and church.

At the time we began our work, however, there was a pervading sense that the investment and rebuilding needed to create such conditions would be too difficult, too complex, and too frightening to undertake. And, as in any community, residents were divided into camps by cultural attitudes and economic backgrounds which provided a brake on the potential for change. There was also a recognition that though much of property was locally owned, there was neither ready capital nor demand to make the necessary improvements.

From the outset, therefore, we realized that revitalization initiatives in Coconut Grove would only be effective if local residents and business were committed to them. Such a commitment would also be essential if the community were to own the process, and eventually take it over. To make this happen community-based organizations would need to work together, instead of against each other. But, early on, at meetings of both small and large groups, we heard every reason why things couldn't or shouldn't happen. For this reason, we saw a need for the whole community to come together and speak in one voice about the future.

Investment happens only when there is good reason to believe conditions will improve. Thus, conditions seldom improve where there are

feuds, resistance, or lack of consensus about how to proceed. Private investors and public agencies generally only place their bets on neighborhoods where they believe investments will appreciate or be appreciated. We therefore had to convince the neighborhood that it would only be able to attract outside assistance if it could be show to a broad base of support.

To address this problem, our first call was to the Coconut Grove Local Development Corporation (LDC). The local HUD office had recommended this organization as one which might benefit particularly from association with the university initiative. The LDC had been successful in building homes in the past, but more recently it had largely transformed itself into a placement agency for the dispersal of city and county affordable-housing funds. Typically, the LDC thus now found itself advising families or individuals on how to repair credit ratings or apply for mortgage and loan assistance.

What CUCD offered the LDC was the chance to move back into the business of building new or rehabilitated housing. To do this, the LDC would only have to become the university's local development partner. Subsequently, it was the LDC that introduced CUCD to a local developer and builder who facilitated our first student-designed affordable home project. And eventually, the linkage between CUCD and the LDC would become essential in applying for grants from foundations and government agencies and encouraging a more broad-based level of university/community collaboration.

As part of our desire to unite the community, we also soon realized that we needed a focus to draw its various elements together. Throughout

Monthly meetings led to the creation of the Coconut Grove Collaborative.

President Shalala shares her hopes at an early community design meeting.

our early contacts there, when we asked how could help, we were often told: "We don't need another charrette — what we need is to know what to do with Grand Avenue." Thus, we adopted Grand Avenue as our first planning initiative, and we immediately invited the community to participate. Through a series of monthly meetings — to which we brought drawings and maps of existing conditions, and at which we recorded community concerns — we began to see a new perspective emerge. It was at this time that the notion of a new organization also surfaced, one that would reflect the membership in all existing organizations. Thus, with the help of a consultant and facilitator, the Coconut Grove Collaborative was born.

There was palpable new energy in the community about this organization. After its creation, efforts to get local people to meetings and to interest politicians and university officials were increasingly successful. Of course, the Collaborative did have its share of growing pains. And it did have to vie for standing with older organizations. But as a result of its efforts, people once again began to talk about community change, rather than improvement of their particular properties or advancement of their particular interests.

GATHERING RESOURCES

With the groundwork set for real projects to take shape, CUCD began to look for sources of funding for community design projects. There were no readily accessible funds within the University of Miami for development purposes. But we were able to set about leveraging the university's connections to generate outside grant funding.

Our first application was to the Office of Community Partnerships at the U.S. Department of Housing and Urban Development for a grant targeted at allowing universities to create Community Outreach Partnership Centers (COPC). We were not successful in this initial application, but we were encouraged to apply again the following year for a different type of University Community Grant, one we were told would be more oriented toward what we wanted to do. In particular, we wanted to apply HUD funding to real building projects, rather than the creation of a new agency.

The second HUD grant we applied for was called a Hispanic Serving Institution Assisting Communities Grant (HSIAC). Through this program we were awarded $400, 000 based on our proposal to complete three tasks: 1) build two affordable homes for first-time homebuyers from the neighborhood; 2) renovate an abandoned building into a mixed-use commercial and residential property; and 3) develop a better framework for the community to articulate and implement general development goals. Overall, we envisioned the purpose of the HUD money as being to create projects that would stimulate other people either living in or passing through the community to improve additional properties. Such a catalytic effort seemed easily attainable within the proposed two-year timeframe, since our partner, LDC, already owned both properties on which the homes would be built, and also owned the mixed-use building which we planned to renovate. In the end, however, the grant had to be extended an extra year to accommodate complications and adjustments in contracts, ownership, partners, scope, and city permits. Despite these pauses and slowdowns, concrete evidence that the university was willing to look for funds and work with existing community organizations had a positive effect on perceptions both inside

Community charrettes and presentations brought concerns and opportunities to light.

Grand Avenue. Live-Work units

and outside West Coconut Grove.

At about the same time, the university also received an invitation to apply for a grant to assist in community revitalization from the local John S. and James L. Knight Foundation. The university offered this opportunity to the CUCD on the basis of our already-existing initiative in West Coconut Grove. The $250,000 planning grant we received from the Knight Foundation in response to our application for a much larger sum then became a significant catalyst for our ability to mobilize the community to begin several other projects.

Ultimately, grant money from the Knight Foundation allowed us to design improvements to a local city park, and to sponsor collaborations between the community and various other divisions within the university — including the School of Communication, the School of Law, the School of Education, and the Departments of Art and History. The primary and most successful outcome of this effort was the series of workshops and reports regarding improvements to Grand Avenue, its streetscape, and adjacent properties.

Overall, through the Knight Foundation and other sources, the university has been able to obtain funding for four main activities in West Coconut Grove: community design projects, community surveys, and two major vision plans — one for Grand Avenue and one for Coconut Grove as a whole. The following four sections describe these initiatives.

COMMUNITY DESIGN PROJECTS

The design studio comprises nearly half of every architecture student's credit in any term. Design problems are generally posed by faculty for students to resolve during the course of the semester. The CUCD has encouraged students and faculty to conceive of design projects in West Coconut Grove and use the neighborhood as a rich source of real design issues, and as a laboratory for learning about community involvement. Each time a studio project is set in West Coconut Grove more insight is gained about the community from reviews with residents and discussion about the success of proposed designs. And as a follow-on to studio work, in several instances funding has been received to build structures originally designed as studio projects.

The following community design projects have occurred over the last few years.

Thomas Ave. House: designed Fall 1999, built Spring 2000. The first student-designed and -built house was sold to a local family, a first-time homebuyer, with the assistance of city grants and a local community development corporation. Such second-mortgage programs are crucial both to keeping new homes affordable and accessible and to increase homeownership for worthy and qualified local families.

Grand Avenue Live-Work Units: designed Fall 2000. Architecture students were asked to develop designs with Caribbean architectural references or a string of substandard lots facing Grand Avenue. This part of Grand Avenue has been considered a prime opportunity for starter omes, featuring an office on the ground floor and residential space in the rear and above. The student designers used add-on wooden balconies to ameliorate required setback constraints.

129

Ace Theater Complex

Carter Street house renovations: Fall 2000. Many abandoned homes in West Coconut Grove had become drug and crack houses before they were finally boarded up by the Miami Police. Today these structures provide important opportunities to extend homeownership programs. Depending on zoning, they can be renovated into one- or two-unit homes. The architecture students produced designs for typical prototype renovations.

3659 Grand Avenue: renovation of mixed-use complex, Spring 2001. A boarded-up, two-story building shell with parking on an adjacent lot was seen as an ideal opportunity to create a small mixed-use project to demonstrate the potential for a building renaissance along Grand Avenue. Numerous student designs were presented to show the benefits of adding on and repurposing the existing building. With a grant from HUD, the university is now helping the owner, the Urban Empowerment Corporation, make this a reality.

Carter Street House: Spring 2001. A local affordable-home developer, Wind & Rain, Inc., has supported University of Miami student design projects over the years. In this case it offered a lot with a large existing oak tree as a design opportunity. The tree and its roots became a key ingredient in the design of a two-story home.

Ace Theater Complex. The subject of a number of architectural class projects and theses over the years, this community landmark has been closed for nearly twenty years, waiting new life. Today it sits adjacent to some vacant land, which suggests the creation of an adjacent courtyard and cultural performance space. This building has great potential to serve as a keystone for the revival of Grand Avenue, but as is typical of many local properties, the family which owns it does not have the funds to rejuvenate it. Nevertheless, they recognize its future potential and past history as an active cinema and auditorium. Many student designs have been presented that illustrate opportunities for this building.

New York St. Townhouses: Spring 2001. A property owned by the Local Development Corporation, zoned for two-family occupancy, was offered to the students as an opportunity to create a new housing prototype. The property owner selected a student design which would create attached townhouses. By joining the units, additional living space could be created in an area normally devoted to side-yard setbacks. The resulting side-by-side houses were spacious, attractive and unique.

St. Matthews Church Fellowship Hall Addition: Spring 2002. Becoming involved in the community and offering the School of Architecture's expertise has led to requests from individuals and organizations to advise on design possibilities. Whenever possible, the CUCD has provided schematic designs for these projects as a way to help property owners begin to envision what might be built. Careful to not take business away from local architects, the work only responds to projects which would not happen if an organization like the CUCD did not initiate the new ideas.

Green Gardens Herb Restaurant and Grocery: Spring 2002. The owner of a nondescript building on Grand Avenue wanted to open a café and shop for his fresh-herbs business. In order to do this, however, he needed to improve his building to attract customers and accommodate a display of products and services. The architecture students designed several schemes to reorient the building and use traditional materials to create a large porch for sitting and sampling beverages and snacks.

Gils' Spot renovation and addition: Spring 2002. An abandoned building at the main intersection in West Coconut Grove posed a difficult problem for architecture students: how to make the most of an existing structure while adding the type of flair that might attract new tenants. The successful solution demonstrated how a shallow, two-story addition could greatly expand usable area on the property. The resulting renovation now promises to spur redevelopment of the three other underused corners of the intersection.

Transit-Oriented Development at Douglas Station: Spring 2003. A

A Transit Oriented Development could provide a landmark and a gateway.

prime gateway property on the main north-south artery entering West Coconut Grove is currently occupied by county welfare offices. The county has offered the property for development gratis, if new development there were to replace its existing 25,000-sq.ft. facility as part of a larger mixed-use development. Since this property is located across the highway from a mass-transit station, it might provide an ideal location for a transit-oriented-development (TOD). So far, the community has turned down designs that it feels are too dense for this site. But the university has prepared schematic studies that show how such a complex might be a tremendous asset if proper planning principles are observed.

COMMUNITY SURVEYS

The second area where CUCD has helped the West Village community and the City of Miami is in producing surveys of physical conditions in West Coconut Grove. Up-to-date maps showing vacant lots, abandoned structures, historic structures, building types, building uses, and even ownership information are extremely important to people interested in increasing active ownership of properties.

Vacant Lot Surveys. Ownership information about vacant lots can help reveal patterns of neglect in a community. Are these properties county or city owned, occupant owned, rented, absentee or local rented, dilapidated or well-kept? Maps can help illustrate all or part of this information, demonstrating the dispersal of any particular quality or condition or use. Such information can also be helpful when trying to identify a particular property's potential for development vs. preservation as part of a park or land trust.

Building Condition Surveys. Such surveys can indicate concentrations of neglect. This information can then be used to develop homeownership programs, renovating programs, and historic assessments. When compared to ownership, accident, and crime data, these surveys may also be a valuable tool for planners, police, nonprofit developers, and sociologists. In another Miami neighborhood, East Little Havana, surveys of architectural features such as porches and picture windows have been correlated to health and crime information to evaluate the role of the environment in community behavior.

Community Assets. Maps showing the assets of a community can be particularly useful to show residents the positive features of their community. Such efforts may be essential in terms of changing negative attitudes and overcoming resistance to change. Positive feedback on what is there, rather than what is not, can help restore pride. In West Coconut Grove, churches are important assets to the spiritual and social structure of the neighborhood. There are twenty-six churches within the project area, and most people know to which church or parish each per son or family belongs.

Historic Building Surveys. It is important to identify historic structures, since they also give residents a sense of pride in their community. In this regard, in West Coconut Grove, Charles Avenue, formerly known as Evangelist Street, was one of the first paved streets in Miami. - Recognition of historic buildings along Charles Avenue suggests the possibility of designating an historic district to attract visitors to its uniqu e accumulation of extant Dade County pine homes.

Entry to Grand Avenue at US1.

Grand Avenue heading East.

THE GRAND AVENUE VISION PLAN

As already mentioned, CUCD's major early achievement in the neighborhood was the development of a Grand Avenue Vision Plan. This was produced over eight months of meetings between the University of Miami School of Architecture and the business and property owners of Coconut Grove.

The desire for such a plan originally grew out of the "next steps" suggested in the City of Miami's Coconut Grove Planning Study of 1996. Following these recommendations, the Grand Avenue Vision Plan was intended to present a vision for a revitalized street of mixed "residential, office and commercial" uses. Toward this end, it incorporated many recommendations for zoning changes, streetscape improvements, and measures that would increase security and livability. In this effort, special attention was taken to recognize the character and scale of existing buildings, and suggest ways to improve or replace them that might allow the street to regain its quality as a focus of neighborhood activity.

Design Process. The Grand Avenue Vision Plan emerged from a fourstage process, which proceeded incrementally from data gathering and analysis, to schematic design, to community meetings, and final design. As part of this gradual approach, presentations were made to the community each month, so that a design direction could emerge in a way that was not threatening to community members. Indeed, at the critical moment when a draft plan was submitted to the community, there was little objection to its specifics — with the exception of a few property owners who had hoped their properties would be recommended for more intense development.

Creation of the report involved surveys of such important parameters as zoning, ownership, parking, and historic conditions. These led to a block-by-block reconsideration of buildings and vacant properties to identify those most likely to be rebuilt or improved in coming years. In several instances, the report suggested the aggregation of smaller lots to create the potential for larger buildings. Development of common parking areas also suggested on properties scattered throughout the area.

Envisioning a Revitalized Grand Avenue. Many people have trouble reading two-dimensional drawings and maps, and newer presentation techniques that involve "fly-through" movies of virtual places are much more successful at explaining spatial improvements. Although we did not have the resources to create such movies, we were able to provide renderings and perspective views of proposed changes at key points along the avenue. Some of these images are included in the accompanying illustrations.

ILLUSTRATIONS

Entry to Grand Avenue at US1. The most traveled entrance to Grand Avenue is from the major Miami artery, US1. This location provides an ideal opportunity to announce the chosen architectural themes of the neighborhood. A tower which speaks to the scale of the roadway would be an appropriate gesture.

Grand Avenue heading East. As Grand Avenue moves eastward there are opportunities to develop buildings several stories higher than are currently there. To build such buildings that can accommodate onsite parking, however, will require the assembly of sites composed of multiple lots. Large buildings can still have a Caribbean style if they are articulated and detailed to feature these elements.

Vision Plan Report and Guidelines. At the conclusion of the eight-month process, maps, drawings and written guidelines were assembled into a final report. This was distributed to the community and to the City of Miami Department of Planning and Zoning. According to the plan recommendations, private developers and landowners would still be responsible for proposing individual building projects. But if the guidelines were adopted by the city, building massing and street-facing architectural details and materials could be significantly controlled. The report also illustrated prototypes for four typical buildings of different uses. These showed how new building projects might implement the ideas in the vision plan. The architectural design guidelines included in the report also illustrated typical features of what was referred to as "Caribbean Style" and "Island Architecture." Some typical elements included shutters and trellises, porches and dormers, balconies and arcades, and even tin roofs in Caribbean colors. The report recommended that incentives be written into the zoning code to allow bonuses or reprieves if such features were incorporated in future project designs.

Implementation. After its completion, the plan was endorsed by the Coconut Grove Collaborative and the Village West Homeowners and Tenants Association. To date, it has also become the basis for new zoning legislation designed to protect and promote the character and scale of the existing street. Recommendations for development in the plan demonstrated this need for new zoning legislation, and the university and the community suggested several specific changes to existing zoning as well as the creation of a special zoning district. These suggestions were subsequently incorporated as a new zoning overlay for the area now approved by the Miami City Commission, with the help of the Department of Planning and Zoning.

The Grand Avenue Vision Plan is also now being assessed, project by project, so that it can become a true and comprehensive implementation plan for the area. As part of this effort, goals and implementation costs for each property must be determined as a precursor to seeking

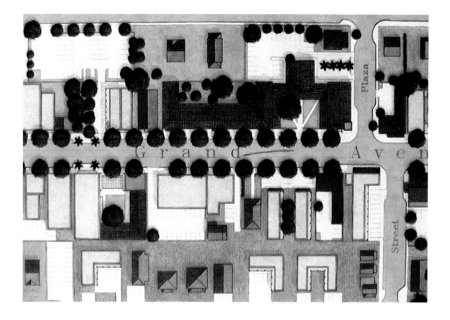

investors and attracting developers to the area.

COCONUT GROVE VISION PLAN

Following the planning effort for Grand Avenue, it became apparent that there was a need to improve and protect the neighborhood as a whole. If redevelopment and revitalization were to occur, it was important that the local community and its resource partners work to identify and preserve unique and important community characteristics.

Among overlay mechanisms employed by the City of Miami is one called the Neighborhood Conservation District. This helps preserve areas with architectural, historical or geographical significance. It was decided then that a second report and vision plan was needed to help the city's Department of Planning and Zoning to implement this strategy to create a Coconut Grove Village West Island District. This second vision plan for the entire area of West Coconut Grove was developed by the CUCD, West Grove stakeholder organizations and community members, University of Miami architecture and law students, and City of Miami urban planners over a nine-month period in 2003 .

Overall, this second effort involved more community meetings and workshops to generate ideas about how the community might be improved in such areas as safety, parks, lighting, landscaping, curbs and drainage, and traffic calming. The culmination of these workshops was a three-day Community Design Workshop. As part of this work, a significant effort was made to identify and seek input from a major stakeholder groups. These eventually came to include the existing business and property owners on Grand Avenue; the Village West Home Owners and Tenants Association; the Island District Merchants

Historic view of Coconut Grove Playhouse

Coconut Grove Vision Plan

Association; and the Coconut Grove Ministerial Council.

All these events were convened and coordinated by the Coconut Grove Collaborative, working primarily through its Design, Planning, Zoning and Historic Preservation Committee. For its part, the University of Miami provided architectural and legal assistance, while the City of Miami helped with the language and logistics of the NCD overlay. The final report included a series of ideas, planning priorities, and even building prototypes. It suggested a number of strategies and resources for implementation. And it proposed specific language for zoning provisions in such areas as designated uses, lot coverage ratios, building massing, and architectural and urban design guidelines.

The text of the report also articulated "Next Steps" for the community and the city might take in the implementation of the vision. These were divided into issues of design, policy and management, and attempted to spell out each party's responsibility in terms of furthering these ideas.

Zoning. As a result of the work, the Miami City Commission voted to designate West Coconut Grove as a Neighborhood Conservation District in 2003. The designation reflects the area's history as an original Miami neighborhood, home to fifth-generation families and an architectural vernacular of Dade County pine shotgun houses. In addition, the city recognized the cultural vitality of the area, as represented by street activity and festivals which reflect the Bahamian heritage of many of its founders.

A number of important zoning changes will result from this designation. Overall, it will limit heights and densities of new development. But it

will also provide zoning incentives for projects that adhere to certain urban design guidelines. In addition, in concert with the community's desire that Grand Avenue once again become a thriving local commercial street, new zoning will allow sidewalk commercial activity along its entire length. Existing zoning only allowed commercial activities along the sidewalk for two of the five blocks along the south side of the street. Existing zoning also allowed residences along only limited portions of another main commercial street, Douglas Road. This too will be changed, so that apartments will be allowed over commercial uses on all the major shopping streets in the district.

Parks and Landscape. The Design Workshop also explored improvements to the parks and landscape features of the neighborhood. There are only two major parks in the neighborhood: Virrick Park at the center of the northern portion, and Armbrister Park at the edge of the southern portion. West Coconut Grove also has significantly less tree cover than surrounding neighborhoods.

The accompanying map illustrates the consensus that developed that no home in Coconut Grove should be further than a three-minute walk from a park of some description, and that shade trees should be planted as soon as possible along streets connecting residential areas to the larger parks. The report also recommended the development of pocket parks or tot lots, and one portion of Margaret Street was identified as the location of a two-block long linear park.

134

Grand Avenue Master plan in progress.

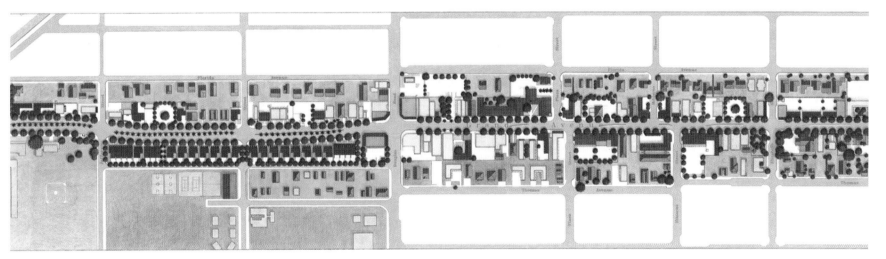

GRAND AVENUE
PROPOSED MASTER PLAN

0   100   200   300   400   500   1,000   1,320 feet

N

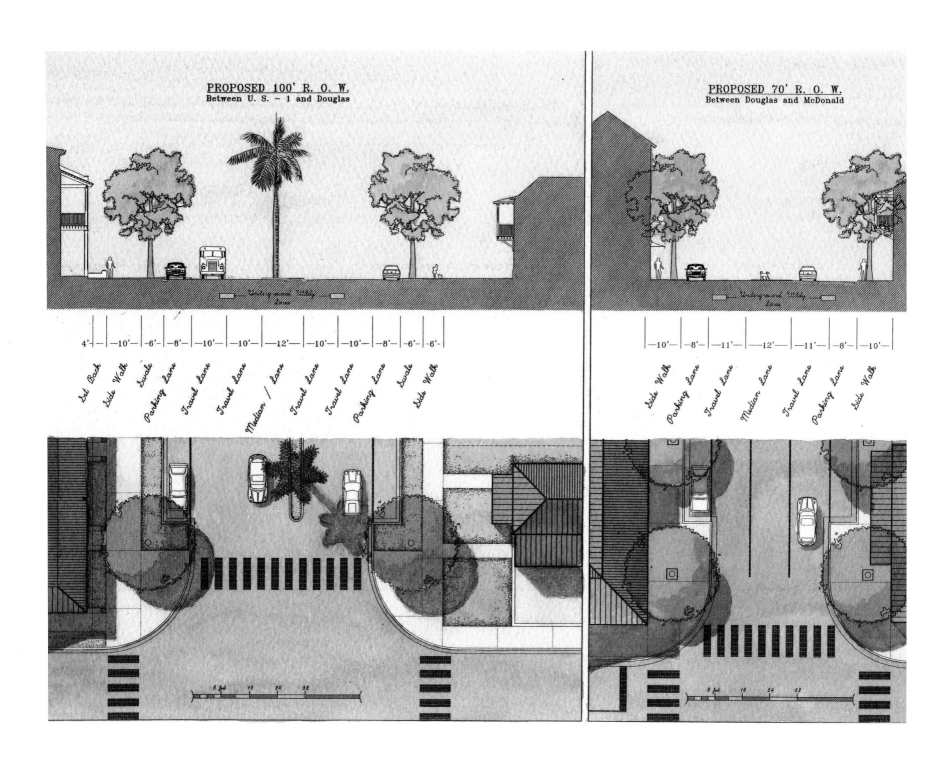

PROPOSED 100' R. O. W.
Between U. S. — 1 and Douglas

PROPOSED 70' R. O. W.
Between Douglas and McDonald

4'	10'	6'	8'	10'	10'	12'	10'	10'	8'	6'	6'

Set Back / Side Walk / Swale / Parking Lane / Travel Lane / Travel Lane / Median / Lane / Travel Lane / Travel Lane / Parking Lane / Swale / Side Walk

10'	8'	11'	12'	11'	8'	10'

Side Walk / Parking Lane / Travel Lane / Median Lane / Travel Lane / Parking Lane / Side Walk

Prototypes for Grand Avenue buildings demonstrate recommended architectural style and buffered parking. Drawings by Eric Vogt

Drawings by Eric Vogt

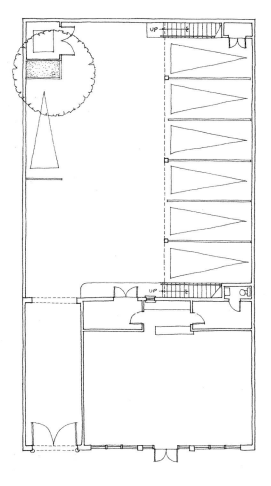

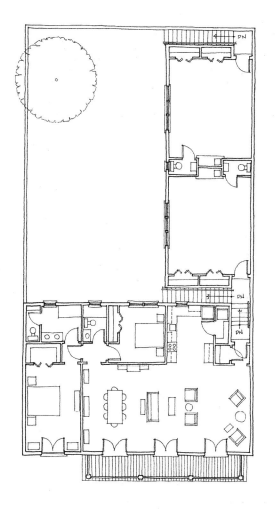

The Building Project

Richard Shepard
University of Miami School of Architecture
Center for Urban and Community Design

Photo: Richard Shepard

From the university's point of view, one of the most important aspects of the work has been to give students a chance to apply classroom learning to real-life situations. The first real opportunity to do this arose as part of a studio in which architecture students were given the task of designing affordable homes for first-time homebuyers in Coconut Grove. At the beginning of the studio, a local developer and builder of simple homes had been drawn into the effort as technical advisor. But the developer eventually suggested that if the students could design a three-bedroom, two-bath home that was 15 feet wide and totaled a maximum of 1,400 square feet, he might be able to build the design on a site where he was already committed to produce a house.

The students who opted for this project were introduced to the community by preparing maps which presented the conditions, uses, historical value, and utility of the buildings and properties in the neighborhood. Through this exercise, they observed firsthand how prevalent vernacular shotgun houses were in the area, and how "the Grove" was defined by a high level of social interaction on its streets and sidewalks. These observations would become important ingredients and measures for the houses they would design.

After mapping the assets of the existing neighborhood, the students were given the program for the house. As work progressed, their designs incorporated its interior requirements. But as a result of their research in the neighborhood, they also placed considerable emphasis on the building's relationship to the yard and the street. Indeed, during design reviews, which were conducted with members of the community, the street frontage (the "outgoing" part of the dwelling), received the most attention.

The most successful of the designs, that for a two-story shotgun house, was designed by a team of four students. They were thrilled to hear that their design would take concrete shape before they graduated. The house design had been produced during the period of one semester (Fall), toward the end of which a local architect had begun advising the students on how to amend their drawings to include systems of plumbing, lighting and wiring, ventilation and structure. But during the winter vacation, the drawings for the house design that was to be built progressed further as the students took responsibility for pushing the drawings through city's permit-approval process and making the

Drawing by Tony Sosa

Photos: Richard Shepard

Grand Avenue

Douglas Road

Thomas Avenue

changes required by plan checkers. Eventually, in late February, their frustration turned to delight as the house received the necessary permits. In the Spring semester, the developer allowed the students to provide the labor and supervision for the construction of the house. Many other students joined in to help build the house, and the sight of construction dirt in the classroom added a new dimension to work at the School of Architecture. Balancing wheelbarrows full of concrete to pour the foundation was a new experience to the students involved. On the brink of graduating with Bachelor of Architecture degrees, they were actually experiencing the materials and methods, sweat and grime, of making a building. The lessons learned would be indelible, and the building left behind would stand as a testament of these young people's commitment to this community.

At the same time, the university began to experience benefits from its effort to make such a project possible. And one of the more significant demonstrations of the breaking down of barriers this project promoted was the decision by the very students whose house design was built to purchase two properties in the neighborhood for their own use.

THREE NEW AFFORDABLE HOUSES

In recognition that students benefit from the experience, and that the community benefits from good prototypes for affordable houses, the School of Architecture decided that the building project should continue as a regular curriculum offering. The success of the work on Grand Avenue plan also helped convince the City of Miami to offer two further vacant lots for development by a team led by the CUCD. Since land prices were already beginning to climb in West Coconut Grove, the city's contribution was extremely important in assuring the affordability of houses produced on these lots. In the Fall semester of 2002 a group of architecture students were assigned to produce three new designs for affordable homes on these target lots. These were further intended to reflect historical building types in the neighborhood. In an introductory exercise, the students studied and documented traditional southern U.S. homes. They were then assigned to reinterpret these to accommodate a three-bedroom, two-bath, 1,300-sq.ft. program. After considerable research, the students arrived at three model house types, updated forms of which might provide the basis for new residences in the area: the bungalow, the dogtrot, and the eyebrow, or conch house.

THE BUNGALOW

Oak Avenue centerline

The Bungalow has the most colorful and lengthy history of the traditional house type. Tracing its origin to simple huts British officers observed in Bengal in India in the 19th century, the Bungalow became the most popular of house types from 1890 to 1930 on the North American Continent.

Typically the Bungalow had no basement, was one or one and a half stories with the upstairs tucked under the roof or dormer of the roof and there is an openness and interrelationship of outdoor and indoor spaces. The strong roof shape served different purposes in different

regions but in the South it protected a spacious porch and served as a comfortable covered place to enjoy evenings breezes and neighbors strolling by.

Our modern Bungalow extends its roof to cover a side entrance and carport and efficiency divides the public rooms and private rooms with a wall down the middle of the house.

Drawings by Hao Hee

THE "DOGTROT"

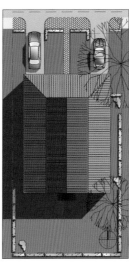

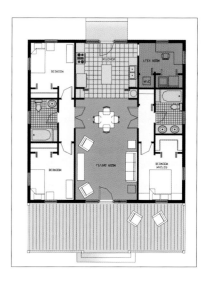

The traditional Dogtrot house consisted of two rooms separated by a breeze way or hall way covered by a common roof. The open passage was used to protect animals from the elements or allow them to run through the house. It could also be the dinning area situated conveniently between the cooking area and the sleeping area.

The Dogtrot house was described by Mark Twain in Huckleberry Finn "It was a double house, and a big open space betwixt their was roofed and floored and sometimes the table was set there in the middle of the day and it was cool comfortable place!!

The contemporary Dogtrot House the students designed for Coconut Grove has kept the idea of an open space in the center, using it for not only dinning but also cooking and sitting. Three bedrooms and two baths flank the central space and the entire 1300S.F. house is covered with a large hipped roof which embraces the front back porches as well.

THE "EYEBROW"

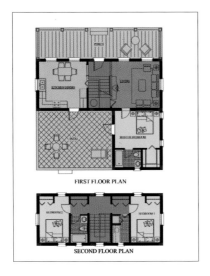

FIRST FLOOR PLAN

SECOND FLOOR PLAN

The "Eyebrow" house was derived from the "I" house, so named due to its narrow profile, one room deep and two stories high. "Eyebrow" because the front windows from the upstairs rooms peer out shielded by a protective roof above. In South Florida such house is also called a "Conch House" to distinguish its higher status from an ordinary one story house or "shotgun shack".

Few true "I" houses remain as many, like this example have addition on the rear to accommodate a larger family and one which chose to show their importance by presenting a more impressive façade to the street.

The narrowness was also well suited to warmer climates and the need for cross ventilation. Our modern adaptation uses the "ell" of the bedroom addition to protect a private "parterre" for family gatherings or dinning in cooler months.

146   *Drawings by Hao Hee*

INTERVIEW WITH ARCHITECTURE STUDENTS

Tony Sosa, Jason Bush and Troy Ballard were students at the University of Miami's School of Architecture from 1995 to 2000. In their last year, they spent the spring to fall semesters designing, permitting and building a house at 3644 Thomas Avenue in western Coconut Grove. Before the project, none of the students had spent any significant amount of time in the Grove, even though they had all lived in the neighboring Coral Gables community. By the end of it, all three ended up being homeowners in the West Grove.

What was the West Grove like when you first went there?

Tony: When we first went into the Grove, I'll be honest with you, everyone was a little nervous. They made it seem like a bigger deal than it was. The school had set up community escorts to walk around with us. They made it more intimidating than it needed to be. But we started spending time there and we grew perfectly comfortable. It wasn't like we were outsiders or anything. We got to the point that we were all so comfortable that we all decided to move there.

In what way was it intimidating?

Tony: Well, we were a bunch or college students with community escorts that were saying, "Be careful; don't go that way." So it was the school, but it was our own preconceptions of the place too. We didn't know the neighborhood, but it was always the neighborhood that you would drive through but kind of roll the windows up. Once we got to know the place, though, we got to become part of the community. It wasn't a big deal at all.

What was the initial concern?

Jason: At one time, crime was an issue in the West Grove, and it had just gotten this label as being kind of a rough neighborhood. I think by the time we actually happened upon it, it wasn't even an issue anymore. I think they were trying to prepare us for being in an inner city neighborhood where something could happen if you weren't careful. But all of our experiences were positive. We never had any problems. It was never an issue.

What appealed to you about the design studio that brought you there?

Troy: I think for all of us, it was the idea that we were actually designing something that was going to be built.

Tony: It was a real project; it wasn't some pie in the sky...We did a lot of school projects that were strictly theory. They were great and we learned a lot from them, but we knew that we were going to be in the real world eventually so we might as well start looking at what's really out that and how to put the stuff together.

And that was valuable?

Tony: It was very valuable for us.

Did the design studio meet your expectations?

Tony: Totally.

Troy: It surpassed our expectations. The program was really a confluence of agendas. For the school, a social agenda; for the developer, a social and financial agenda; for the students, we were looking for something more real. All those agendas merged into one and we began to understand the opportunity for us as volunteers within the community and to be a part of change. I think certainly the school recognized the educational value of what we were getting out of it. For the developer and contractor, it was the recognition of the imagination and the vitality that the students brought to the program and the energy that they brought to the design had a benefit for him.

Can you describe what you did during this studio?

Jason: In the beginning, it was mostly the design process. We came up with a plan that was approved and then we actually went on to permitting. We got our construction documents permitted through the city and then we came out and we built it. We made it happen.

So from start to finish...

Tony: Yup. We built it.

Troy: We designed and built a building. Usually, in school, you just design it on a piece of paper and it never exists beyond that. That's really the story. We designed something real. We permitted it – which is a process in and of itself – and we then we went out and built it.

Would you recommend it to other architecture students?

Jason: Definitely.

Troy: Invaluable experience.

How did it compare with the rest of your educational experiences?

Tony: I speak for myself, and I'm sure that these guys will probably agree. Out of the five years we were there, the two things that will stand out the most is building the house and traveling abroad to Rome. I think it's by far one of the top two things that we did.

Jason: I agree. I think it was a good way to end things. I think it solidified everything that we had learned. You go through five years of architecture and there's a lot of different ways you can take it at the end. Surprisingly enough, after all the money and all the time and all the effort, a lot of people don't get their license to practice architecture. Some people go into interior design; some people go into construction, model building, rendering, development, and even law sometimes. I think that doing this project, everybody took their position and they just continued with it.

So you think it helped point out your strengths or confirm things you were already thinking?

Tony: Probably more confirmed that anything else. We all kind of knew where we were leaning for a long time and it just kind of helped us make sure that that's what we wanted to do.

Jason: It was just real project. You got to see the numbers, the actual process...You got to see the construction, design, permitting and what you need to actually get something designed and built. All in all, it was a pretty good experience.

Has the experience affected the way you see your career developing?

Tony: I think we all kind of stuck to it. I think we all went out and did in our careers what we wound up doing in the project. Jason went into construction. Troy went to development. I went to design.

Troy: It's interesting the direction the four of us went. None of us do the same thing [as the others] now, but it's definitely related. The seeds of a lot of that go back to when we were in school. Probably that last year of school was really a springboard of our careers.

Some of you decided to buy homes in the West Grove. How did you come to that decision?

Jason: We all decided to buy homes in the West Grove.

Troy: We recognized the potential of the Grove and really felt that it was tremendously undervalued. We felt that the seeds of change already existed in the neighborhood. We'd spent over a year already in the Grove and were already excited about the changes that were happening. We wanted to further be a part of it. That, coupled with the desire to be property owners after we graduated, is what led us to the Grove.

Were you considering any other neighborhoods?

Troy: Not really.

Tony: I went all over Miami.

Tony, so the Grove was not your first choice?

Tony: No, it was not...I was getting married and we were looking for a house. We were just looking all over the place. I was working in Fort Lauderdale at the time, so I was trying to find something a little further

Photo: Douglas Robbins

north. But I always hung out with these guys and I always loved the Grove, and then an opportunity came up where a house down the street from them went for sale. [My wife, Isa, and I] went to look at it and we bought it.

How would you describe your relationship with your neighbors?

Jason: The West Grove is full of very interesting people...

Tony: Yes...

Jason: People were always very friendly. Overall, I'll say it's an interesting neighborhood to be in. I come from a small town in western Massachusetts. It's good and it's bad because it seems that everybody knows you, everybody knows your business, and everybody's talking to everybody about your business. This is a significant neighborhood down here. In a city that's so spread out and populated like Miami, you can have a neighborhood where people actually know their neighbors and speak to one another and say hello.

That seems like a long way from your first impression, when the neighborhood was intimidating.

Tony: Exactly.

Has the neighborhood changed since you got there?

Tony: We've always been friendly with our neighbors and they welcomed us from day one. It's been great.

Troy: And our opinion of the neighborhood was always strong going in because we'd spent a year building a house there and being involved with the community there. Our opinions of the West Grove were already great. Certainly, the neighborhood has begun to improve more and more and the speed of that change is quickening.

Tony: Property values have skyrocketed. I don't think I could afford to buy a house here now. I couldn't afford my house now. Property values have tripled.

Troy: In some cases, it was undervalued. Now, there is much more interest in the area. A lot of people are investing, which makes the prices climb very quickly.

Do you think the university should be involved in the community?

Troy: I think they are. I think the university has been really a leader in making some of the changes there. They've shown a willingness to work with the private sector, with the community and with government to make changes. I think the university has done a great job, and I think they will continue to...When it comes right down to it, five years ago, we got involved through the university and through a private developer, Andy Parish. We're all still involved in the West Grove.

In this multidisciplinary effort, did you learn anything from the other departments or students and from their way of thinking?

Jason: The history department did different oral histories of different families in the West Grove. The photography department went around and photographed a lot of the old buildings, a lot of the people to go along with the oral histories. They had a big exhibition on campus. It was really great.

Troy: One of the experiences I remember very well is speaking with (Coconut grove community leader) Thelma Gibson. The amazing thing about it was because the history department was doing work and the photography department was doing work, I really had no idea how fresh and how recent some of the segregation was and some of the civil rights issues were. Certainly, her husband was a big player in that, and she's been a big player in that. I remember very vividly meeting with her and listening to her stories and realizing that this woman who is about the age of my grandma experienced a completely different environment than the one we grew up in today. As young people, we tend to think that what we're going through today is pretty similar to what our parents went through, but it's not that way at all. I think that for us, what the history department was doing and what the photography department was doing – the oral histories that they took and our exposure to that through this program – was just eye opening in many ways. I had no idea how close all of that history was. This definitely made a difference.

Tony: It was interesting to see from the point of view of a different culture. It was good for all of us to see somebody else's point of view.

Jason: And there's also the richness of the Bahamian culture that exists there, from the food to the music to the hairstyles to the architecture. A year doesn't go by that we don't go to the Goombay Festival, which we were exposed to really when we were in this program.

Tony: We'd never even heard of it before then.

Jason: Yeah. I think we did develop an appreciation of these things that

we probably wouldn't have without this experience. And hopefully, the other students, the history students and the photography students, got an appreciation of the environment and how that can affect change as well. We certainly got something from it.

Photo: Richard Shepard

Learning Right from Wrong

Anthony R. Parrish, Jr., President
Wind & Rain, Inc.

In March of this year 2004, Wind & Rain celebrated its 10th Anniversary. Reflection on our first decade prompted reflection on our initial principles. Starting from discussions in 1994 around the dining room table of a friend, Wind & Rain formulated a basic strategy for turning an impoverished African-American neighborhood, the West Grove, into a prosperous, vital, crime-free community without gentrifying it. This is where we began:

1. To build single family detached homes for ownership by first-time homeowners living and working in the community.
2. To make sure the homes are big enough, and designed well enough to appreciate in value over time.
3. To sell the homes for a price and with a financing package so that the monthly payment is "the equivalent of rent."
4. To do all this without any hand-outs from government coming to Wind & Rain, and to still make a profit.

If Wind & Rain could successfully do these four things by even building just a few houses, we sincerely thought the light would then shine into the hearts and minds of both the public and the politicians and we'd be building a hundred "affordable" homes a year or more. After all, as the saying goes, "Build a better mouse trap and the world will beat a path to your door."

Ten years later, Wind & Rain's has a record of accomplishments of which it is justly proud. We are the first for-profit entity to build new houses in the neighborhood in thirty years, the first to build a new office building and a new retail building in fifty years. We created, along with the

University of Miami School of Architecture and the newly formed Coconut Grove Collaborative, a Neighborhood Conservation District. Most importantly, thirteen new homeowners, each of whom started with a $3,000 down payment, now have combined equity in their homes in excess of $2,000,000.

Yet, despite these accomplishments, Wind & Rain has little more momentum to build new affordable homes than when it started. The "better mouse trap," while lauded by the press and community leaders, has attracted no real political support. The subsidized "soft 2nd" mortgage funding—upon which the Wind & Rain model depends to make its houses affordable to low-to-moderate income families—is still very difficult to come by. Even more disappointingly, the thirteen new Wind & Rain homes, and the noticeable community-wide improvement that they represent, have inadvertently provoked a wave of gentrification that now threatens this small historic Bahamian community with skyrocketing rents and an explosion of "McMansions."

In looking back over this decade of hard but rewarding work in the community, Wind & Rain has learned some important lessons that it can take with it to other communities as well as share with other affordable housing providers. Sticking to our core principles has certainly helped us realize many of our goals, but a balanced reflection on both the achievements on which we must capitalize and the lessons that we must learn is a productive step towards sustained positive involvement in the community.

Open-air Grand Restaurant (demolished) 3600 Block of Grand Avenue. 1961 photo courtesy of David Blumenthal

THINGS WE DID RIGHT

DO WELL BY DOING GOOD

From the start, Wind & Rain was going to be a different type of home-builder. It was going to be a "for profit" entity that in many ways acted a lot like a "not for profit." William J. Levitt, the creator of Levittown, the inventor of the great homeowning American middle class back in the '50's, was our model: Build a good house that will go up in value, sell it for "the equivalent of rent" by taking advantage of government backed financing (in Levitt's time it was the "GI Bill"), and make a nice profit, not "per house" necessarily, but by building a lot of them. Habitat for Humanity also shares much of this same philosophy, but plows all of its revenues back into more self-generated "subsidized" mortgages for its next round of new low-income homeowners. Wind & Rain wanted to go the "for profit" route because we didn't want to have to enlist and be responsible to any board of directors, and because we believed then and still do that the only economic engine powerful enough to build the thousands if not millions of new homes needed right now in this coun-try is private, profit-driven enterprise.

GOOD DESIGN IS WORTH EVERYONE'S WHILE

The most cost effective thing any affordable homebuilder can do is to hire a good architect whose heart is into good design. Everything but the house finishes (e.g., the tile work, lighting, floor coverings, win-dows) costs the same, whether you are building a $1,000,000 house or one that sells for under $100,000. The cinder block, the water pipes,

the paint, the stucco, the drywall--all are the same price per sq. ft. Wind & Rain's general contractor, Mario Benitez, taught us early on that to make a house cost less, you generally must build a smaller house, but reducing the size of a house by half may only save you 25% off the price of a house because of the other relatively fixed costs, such as land costs, insurance, surveys and permit fees. Wind & Rain has always been com-mitted to building "enough house to go up in value"—which means no depressing institutional "shoe boxes"—so the trick was to build a cost-effective spacious 3 BR/2BA distinctive house that enhanced the neighborhood and which would serve the families that needed them.

By great good fortune Wind & Rain had just the architect for the task in Marilyn Avery. Marilyn came up with our initial "Caribbean" design, which was basically a square house with a large open porch across the entire front. Why square? Because a house of 1600 sq. ft. that is 40' X 40' costs 25% less to build than a 1600 sq. ft. house that is 80' X 20'. If you don't see why immediately, you are in good company: many of the University of Miami's undergraduate architects, who in 1999 became Wind & Rain's "think tank," didn't see why either. The reason is that the square house has 160 linear feet of walls, while the rectangular one has 200 linear feet. The most useful other way to save on construction cost without shrinking the livable area is by eliminating hallways. The U of M students became experts at that.

We had known the Dean of Miami's School of Architecture, Elizabeth Plater- Zyberk, for years and were well aware of her reputation for "New Urbanism" community design. She had mentioned that the University had just been chosen to host a "Henry Luce Chair" that could impact what Wind & Rain was doing in the West Grove but only if we could help persuade the recipient of the Luce Chair, one Samina Quraeshi, to select the West Grove as a "study area." After meeting Professor Quraeshi at a local Cuban restaurant, we determined immediately that this dynamic visionary Pakistani educator was not going anywhere but the West Grove.

Samina, together with architect Marilyn Avery and Samina's architect husband Richard Shepard, soon convened a workshop at the University's Center for Urban & Community Design under Professor Shepard's tutelage. The aim was to design a livable affordable house that could fit on a "substandard" 25' X 100' wide lot, of which there are many in Miami's poorer neighborhoods. Already we had one strike against us due to the long and narrow lot which would force us away from the efficient square house design. Strike two was the City setback requirements: the house's "footprint" could be no larger than 15' X 60' so that the house would have to be 2 story.

How does one design three bedrooms, two baths, a living room, dining room, a laundry room, two porches and a stairway into a 13' 8" wide (inside measurement) space and still make it roomy and affordable and attractive? The answer is that you eliminate all the hallways you can, and have 30 architecture students, as a team, figure out how to use every square inch of floor space. Then you have those same students help build it from the ground up.

COMMUNITY BUILDING

There is simply no way of avoiding the race issue when a group of mostly white people, well intentioned or not, arrive to "do something" in a predominantly African-American neighborhood. The West Grove in 1994 when we built the first Wind & Rain house was certainly in excess of 90% black occupied, even if the percentage of black ownership of the real estate was much less, probably around 50% overall. Not all of the residents were low income either. As one of Miami's oldest neighborhoods, a lot of the houses were large, well kept, and owned by quite well-to-do families. Even so, the per family income averaged out to something like $12,000 in 1994. And most of the renters were just barely getting by and living under very marginal conditions.

Wind & Rain came into this largely forgotten neighborhood with a straightforward plan. We dealt with the race issue by building homes for ownership rather than rentals, and, with the assistance of the local community development corporation, by actively recruiting and assisting local residents to become the new homeowners.

Wind & Rain discovered to its delight that no matter how "bad" a block was because of drug dealing, illegal dumping, or non-existent code enforcement, it only took two to three new homeowners per street to completely turn that block around. And it only took 15 new scattered site houses in the 45 blocks of West Grove to awaken the whole City of Miami to the renaissance of the community.

Unfortunately, the City's real estate speculators also were awakened to the possibility of acquiring lots and houses at 1950's prices unadjusted for inflation. At this critical juncture, again Professors Shepard and Quraeshi stepped into the breech with timely assistance.

As the McMansion builders began to snap up duplex lots from absentee owners, and the commercial properties began rapidly to change hands as well financed investors made increasing offers to longtime owners, the need for a community wide vision plan became increasingly evident. Building upon the work done by the Duany Plater-Zyberk firm for the City of Miami Coconut Grove Planning Study in the mid '90s, the Center for Urban & Community Design's students surveyed the entire West Grove, documenting its existing structures and infrastructure, and analyzing its strengths and weaknesses for being "reinvented" as a drug free, prosperous community while still retaining its residents.

Working at a furious pace over several semesters, the CUCD students

Super Butcher Shop (now Bernice's Soul Food Restaurant) and Pine Inn (still existing) 3500 Block of Grand Avenue. 1961 photo courtesy of David Blumenthal

generated a Vision Plan for Grand Avenue and an overall Plan for "Village West Island District," a new name picked by vote of the residents. With the community's endorsement generated over months of community design charettes led by Professor Shepard and his students together with the newly formed Coconut Grove Collaborative (an umbrella group comprised of most of the existing organizations and groups in the West Grove), the Grand Avenue Vision Plan was adopted and codified as part of the City's Municipal Code, just in the nick of time to prevent high rise development on Grand Avenue that would have been allowed under the old Code. The Plan for Village West Island District encompassing the residential portions of the neighborhood is being reviewed by the City for implementation as of this writing.

These Vision Plans were designed not only to thwart shortsighted developers, but also to instill rejuvenated pride in the community so that the local residents would not take the offers to sell being thrust into their faces. Part of the task is educational. Families, who for generation after generation have never seen their homes appreciate in value, need to be convinced that their homes are indeed valuable as something more than just shelter, and that the real estate speculator offering them ten times what their grandparents had paid was in fact offering much less than the true value. Then they need a primer in real estate financing—that you don't need to sell to tap into the growing equity in your home. And most important, they need to feel that pride of place that comes with a community that is regaining its health after decades of drugs and crime, of having the neighborhood high school eliminated by desegregation mandates, and being ignored by political leaders, City administrators, and police and code enforcement.

As Professor Quraeshi has observed, this task is made the more difficult when "...what unites a group of people is the trauma of history, not the pride of place it is supposed to infuse into the neighborhood. How then should we, as community builders, constructively engage with the past?"

There are no easy answers to this question, and the unequal financial resources within and without the community load the equation in favor of gentrification, which Wind & Rain defines as the displacement of one socio-economic group by another with more financial resources, and not necessarily as blacks being replaced by non-blacks. To date, exactly none of Wind & Rain's homebuyers has sold out, even though some have been offered in excess of $250,000 for houses purchased from us ten years or less ago for as little as $77,000. As our very first homebuyer, postal worker Cheryl Ogletree said recently: "Where would I go that I would like as much?" Exactly.

THINGS WE DID WRONG

MISSED EDUCATIONAL OPPORTUNITY

Looking back at the major successes we had with the University of Miami's School of Architecture, the one thing we know we did wrong was not to require the University of Miami administration to support the studio Design/Build House project financially with hard dollars, even if such support was only to the tune of $10,000. While we had Dean Plater-Zyberk's support, the project never had any "investment" on the part of the University's administration. This meant that when the next studio class assembled, we were not able to replicate and build upon the previous year's success, despite the fact that the 2nd year class was oversubscribed by new students anxious to begin a new "hands on" design/build house with Wind & Rain.

Why this failure? Because the overwhelming success of the first studio project, which many of the students said was the most intense, rewarding and fun course they took in the whole architectural curriculum, had created a backlash from other faculty members who did not believe students should be involved in real world projects at such an early point in their architectural careers. Furthermore, since the University administration had not put any money into the first project, it saw no reason to put any funding into the second round, even though the first project had been a success for the students. Wind & Rain needed the University to put some dollars into the 2nd project because we had learned that student involvement, due to the learning element, slowed the whole homebuilding process down. In addition, lot prices had begun to climb rapidly in the neighborhood. With a very restricted profit margin to keep the house affordable, the "time is money" adage had proven true in the first studio. The University did not respond.

What an opportunity missed by the University, and by Wind & Rain. Just ask the family living in the student designed and built house on Thomas Avenue. And just ask any of those lucky first studio participants, two of whom after graduation bought houses in "Village West Island District" where they are now working and raising their families.

MISSED ECONOMIC OPPORTUNITY

From the start in 1994 we knew the West Grove was going to get "whiter" sometime. It had to. The community had shrunk from over 10,000 residents in 1950 to approximately 2500 by 1994. Vacant lots abounded where houses once stood. Property values when adjusted for inflation had decreased as much as 80%. In those same 44 years, the rest of Coconut Grove, North, South and Center, had seen its property values in real dollars appreciate 500% and more. The West Grove was a vacuum, and nature abhors those. It was just amazing that the community still existed at all as a primarily low income African-American community, so well located and surrounded on all sides by much wealthier communities.

As we got to know the residents, we realized that this Bahamian heritage community still existed partly because of its deep historical roots, kept alive by the many churches and schools in the community. The other reason for its existence was fear on the part of outsiders-there were crime statistics justifying the wisdom "Don't stop at the light at Grand and Douglas." Wind & Rain did more than its part to change that climate of fear. We built houses for homeownership on drug ridden streets and those streets got better almost overnight. We built the first office building in 50 years on Grand Avenue and suddenly everyone else wanted one, too. We supported a new vision for Grand Avenue with wide sidewalks and tree lined medians and then the City and County found funding to implement the vision. What we didn't do was adequately plan ahead for the onslaught of cash that would be thrown at the unprepared residents for their real estate once things started to improve. We could have, too, by somehow finding a community-friendly investment group to buy the properties owned by the Blumenthal Trust.

The Blumenthal family had owned many properties, including stores, apartment buildings, single family homes, duplexes and quadruplexes, from the 1930's onward. They had been meticulous in their maintenance. By the year 2000, there were less than 100 historic wooden "shotgun" houses left standing in the West Grove. Of these, maybe 70 were in good condition. Of these, probably 90% were "Blumenthals."

The Blumenthals had also been excellent landlords for generations of West Grovites, from founding patriarch Max, to Elliott, to Maurice, to great grandson David, keeping the rents low, helping families in need, forgiving rent when necessary, even paying out of their own pocket for the first water main to go down Grand Avenue. Then in 2001, for a variety of reasons, the Blumenthal Family Trust decided to sell all of its 87 properties.

David Blumenthal brought the whole "package" to Wind & Rain with an asking price of $12 Million for the individual properties, but of $8.5 Million for a bulk sale. The existing rents would support a purchase price of $7 Million but, as David pointed out, the rents were way below what they could and should have been.

We were not able to raise the $8.5 Million even by meeting with some very wealthy investors, or by taking the deal to several Foundations.

None of the people or organizations we contacted seemed to believe this real estate was valuable and under priced. The long history of stagnation and dysfunction was too well known. Neither was Wind & Rain successful in its efforts to buy all of the Blumenthal residential units with state housing subsidies by pledging to keep the units "affordable" for 10 to 15 years-we just did not have a strong enough financial track record. If we had been able to purchase these units, some of the families renting in the community would have had at least a 10 year respite while they adjusted to the fact that their units were becoming valuable to others willing and able to pay more rent-the "gentrification" that everyone feared.

The Blumenthals proceeded to sell off their properties one by one, taking less than a year to do it, and they got close to their asking price. After selling 14 of the residential units to existing long-time tenants for half of their fair market value, the Blumenthal Trust sold the rest of the properties to a wide variety of small investors, gathering momentum with each new "comparable." It was like gasoline on a fire by the end of the year. Many of the properties changed hands again, then again, and then yet again. With each new landlord, the rents went up. Some of those families with month-to-month leaseholds saw their rents double or even triple in less than a year. The bulk sale that David Blumenthal had offered to Wind & Rain for $8.5 Million was now worth an estimated $25 Million less than three years later. Some developers were now planning "high rise" condominiums on assemblages of properties, including many of the former Blumenthal properties. Inevitable development? Or a missed opportunity to slow and control speculation and gentrification? In truth: some of both.

Meanwhile, those families who owned their own homes (including Wind & Rain's 13 families) were seeing 50 years of deferred appreciation arrive on their doorsteps almost overnight. This was a good thing overall. Why shouldn't African-Americans see their homes increase in value just like everyone else in Coconut Grove? And with the State's 3% cap on increases in tax assessments for homestead properties, the increasing real estate taxes would be bearable for most, especially when they realized the value of their homes was going up 50% per year and more.

MISSED POLITICAL OPPORTUNITY

Our greatest disappointment is this: After 10 years of hard work, and proving beyond doubt that construction of new houses for homeownership by existing residents is the key to turning around a decaying neighborhood without displacing the families living there, Wind & Rain has never been able to get the local politicians (with a few notable exceptions) to give more than token support to homeownership. We have come to the conclusion that when it comes to disbursing public money, the politicians are more willing to give large amounts to the few (as with large rental apartment buildings), than to give smaller amounts to the many (as happens with homeownership subsidies). It's easier to do the former, and a lot easier to get campaign contributions.

It is certainly true that you need $30,000 to $40,000 in taxpayer subsidy (in the form of a "soft 2nd" mortgage) to bring the monthly payment on a $100,000 house to the "equivalent of rent" for a low-to-moderate income family. But government, at local, state and federal levels, supports rental subsidy programs that cost the taxpayers far more if you do the math, without even taking into account the intangible benefits (fewer police calls, better school performance, cleaner streets, and on and on) to the community that homeownership brings.

Wind & Rain is certainly not advocating doing away with rental subsidies. We could make a better case philosophically for doing away with government housing subsidies of any kind, including fully deductible mortgage interest on a second home (and partial deductibility on a third vacation home!) that wealthy Americans enjoy. Government also gives federal tax credits for building or renovating rental apartment complexes. It gives Section 8 rental vouchers, sometimes well over $1,000 per month, to absentee landlords, some of whom never maintain their properties. And local government floats tax exempt bond issues for other things, like building sports stadiums. So the question isn't so much about subsidies as it is about priorities.

That being said, all people need shelter, and not all are ready for home-ownership. With political will, each community could hold public hearings each year to calculate how many new houses it needs, both rental and homeownership, and what level of income would be required to qualify to buy the homeownership units. Then it could set the crite-ria-even if it's a lottery-to select the lucky families to own those houses. Private enterprise could competitively build and sell them. Is it too much to ask the mayor of a city as poor as the City of Miami, or the mayor of a county as poor as Miami-Dade County, to say: "Building homes for homeownership for the working poor of this community is my No. 1 priority"-- and mean it?

It is not bleeding soft-heartedness to advo-cate this. It is simply common sense. With the arguable exception of education, home-ownership helps more than any other single thing to build wealth, community pride, and stable families. Whoever you are, think about how different your own life would have been if your family's status had been permanently changed from homeowner to renter or vice versa.

IN HINDSIGHT

It may be that a good part of the reason Wind & Rain's "better mouse-trap" has failed to attract more political assistance is due to its founder's bull headedness. Instead of focusing on the purity of the Wind
158 & Rain paradigm, flexibility might have won more support. As one very

successful Miami developer said: "People may admire what you do, but they respect you only if it also makes money."

Wind & Rain might have made a lot more money if we had bought 50 vacant lots for $5,000 to $15,000 each when we could have back in 1994. Then maybe we could have built a few rental units, or even a few houses for sale, and then just waited for prices to go up. On the other hand, maybe it was Wind & Rain's 13 new homeowners themselves who caused the property boom by taking charge of their neighborhood.

In any case, the voluminous publicity Wind & Rain has gotten over the years is undoubtedly partly responsible for a new City of Miami home-ownership program. This initiative is making available "soft 2nd" mortgages of $40,000 each to thirty low-to-moderate income families buying 2BR/2BA condominiums in East Little Havana. Each subsidized mortgage is totally forgiven if the family lives in the unit for 30 years. One commissioner said at the ribbon cutting: "We are very proud to have supported this development because homeownership brings pride to the entire community and homeowners become more active citi-zens." Wind & Rain could not have said it any better.

Pure Gas station (now offices) 3500 Block of Grand Avenue. 1961 photo courtesy of David Blumenthal

Oral Histories
West Grove Thematic Quotes

Gregory W. Bush
University of Miami School of Arts & Sciences
Department of History

BURDINES: TRYING ON CLOTHES

You didn't have to go downtown to shop. Later on, even when I got going and went downtown to shop, you couldn't try on anything in the stores, and so you didn't want to shop there. I could always remember the only place that had Girl Scout uniforms was Burdine's. So I had to go down there and get a Girl Scout uniform. Come home and try it on. And if it didn't fit, then you had to take it back. They'll take it back, but you couldn't try it on in the store, which I thought was, you know, pretty ludicrous to have to take it home, try it on and then bring it back.

Thelma Anderson Gibson

Photo: Jennifer Gilliam

RELATIONSHIP TO/ISOLATION OF BLACK COMMUNITIES

[A] bicycle was an integral part of every family's material possessions. My bicycle was not only for fun but it was also very crucial to my employment. . .I had to open the church every morning before going to school, which means I had to get up, go up the church open it up, front doors, and the, not all the windows but, every other window or so. It would stay open all day, until I went back in the evening time to close it after work. I was paid twenty dollars a month, which included keeping the church clean, the grass cut, and ringing the bells for services. That was a lot of money in those days, twenty dollars a month.
Reverend Austin Cooper

Everybody in the house had bicycles. We could ride back and forth, but I could not ride my bicycle to school. Our house is so built that we had a garage ... under the kitchen floor that we would [keep] the bicycles in there every night, and he would take them out in the morning for us. I remember riding my bicycle in, we were just 10th graders by that time, Overtown and we would ride over down town. If we wanted to buy

anything, then one of us would look after the bicycles and one would go in, or two would go in and get whatever we wanted from there, come back, and we would ride.
Vernika Silva

INABILITY TO USE WATER: VIRGINIA KEY

We went over to Virginia Key because you could not use Cranden Park in those days. Our church would sponsor beach parties over on Virginia Key. Some were held in the daytime, some were held in the evening time, but always under very good supervision. Mosquitoes would drive you mad over there because there was all that water very heavily infested with mosquitoes. That was the beach that we had. . . If I recall there may have been, there were a couple of drownings. I can't verify that, but I do believe of having heard there were some drownings years ago. If there were lifeguards there probably were just one or two. You know, this was good enough for those neighborhoods.
Reverend Austin Cooper

Photo: J.J. Gama-Lobo

Designing Healthy Communities
The Culture-Centered Science of Built Environment, Behavior and Health

Jose Szapocznik
University of Miami School of Medicine

Arnold R. Spokane
Lehigh University

Joanna Lombard, and Frank Martinez
University of Miami School of Architecture

Craig Mason
University of Maine

Scott C. Brown
University of Miami

Maria Cristina Cruza-Guet, and Rachel-Brandt Greenfeld
Lehigh University

The West Coconut Grove Project, the topic of the present volume, is a powerful example of the culture-sensitive redesign of urban ethnic communities. This novel project preserves and restores the character of West Coconut Grove, a predominantly Caribbean urban enclave. An interdisicplinary undertaking, the Coconut Grove project incorporates the views of architecture, law, medicine, history, art, and communications and parallels intervention trends in the social, behavioral and medical sciences which are increasingly conducted from a culture-centered (Szapocznik & Kurtines, 1993), or culture-sensitive perspective (Pick, Poortinga, & Givaudan, 2003). This culture-sensitive approach implies that when designing or redesigning communities planners incorporate the increasingly clear, fundamental, differences in the social processes characteristic of different cultures (Ji, Peng, & Nisbett, 2000). New findings on the centrality of these cultural differences now requires that community interventions weight these socio-cultural factors as heavily, if not more heavily, than considerations in community design (Pick et. al., 2003). There is, in such projects, then, an imperative for close collaboration with community organizations and courageous individual residents who represent those cultures in the community.

The inclusion of built environment features and characteristics that reflect the culture of origin of residents recreates an environment familiar and supportive of their cultural uniqueness. As this chapter will show, the interaction of the built environment and the social environment of a neighborhood can affect both the physical and the mental health of its residents.

The West Grove Project, is spearheaded by the Coconut Grove Collaborative---a community-based organization and the University of Miami's Center for Urban and Community Design. The project emphasizes the restoration and redesign of distinctive homes such as the "Shotgun" house, the "Dogtrot" or breezeway house and the "Eyebrow" or conch-two story design, structures that are of architectural as well as socio-cultural importance (Shepard, 2002). As an educational experience the West Grove Project is exemplary, because students provided much of the design input.

The "vernacular architecture" of the West Grove serves as a cultural marker of the Caribbean way of life. Built environment markers such as unique architectural styles, carry mixed associations---usually positive creating cultural familiarity or "sense of place" ---sometimes negative. In spite of their architectural significance the "shotgun" houses in West Coconut Grove serve as reminders to locals of the evils of the slave trade and thus carry negative connotations (Quareshi, personal communication, 2004). Thus, understanding which aspects of a culture contribute positively to a positive sense of place is more complex than might be assumed.

Poverty and low socioeconomic status have clear associations with health (Srinivasan, OFallon, & Dearry, 2003). This connection is not necessarily absolute, however. As Earls and his colleagues have demonstrated (Sampson, Raudenbush & Earls, 1997) the social and community structures in a poor neighborhood have crucial buffering effects on the well-being of inhabitants. Poor neighborhoods with strong collective efficacy do not have the devastating social outcomes typically associated with poverty and low SES. The strains associated with low socioeconomic status, then, can be buffered by the redesign of the built environment in ways that strengthen the beneficial effects of positive environments in our socially diverse cities. The relationship between the built environment, behavior and health, then, is a complex interplay between individual behavior, the context in which that behavior occurs, and the health consequences related to both behavior and environment. This chapter explores the relationship between built environments behavior and health from an interdisciplinary perspective.

Three goals of the present chapter are: (a) to review five prominent health issues affecting urban communities that are related to the built environment, (b) to describe the redesign possibilities emanating from these five health concerns, and (c) to outline a research and theory agenda for the new interdisciplinary science of Built Environment, Behavior and Health.

This new field of inquiry we call Built Environment Behavior and Health combines the theoretical perspectives, methodological tools, and practical intervention strategies of architects and urban planners, behavioral scientists, physicians and epidemiologists, public health scientists, bioscientists, engineers and economists. Working collaboratively within diverse urbancultural environments, these pioneering professionals are making fundamental advances in theory, research methodology, and application in community design. The underpinnings of Built Environments Behavior and Health include principles of New Urbanism (Duany & Plater-Zyberk, 1992), models of social ecology (Bronfenbrenner, 1979), theories of cross-cultural behavior, geomapping, including GPS systems, and new statistical methods for nesting individual participants within residential blocks or neighborhoods as allowable in hierarchical linear modeling (Bryk & Raudenbush, 2002). We are now able to study the behavior of individuals in the array of built environments these persons inhabit at a level of methodological sophistication never before possible.

Pertinent public health data (House Landis & Umberson, 1988) confirm that the social processes that occur in urban environments affect the health of inhabitants and these data underscore the fundamental design principles of the New Urban Charter (Congress of the New Urbanism, 2000). Health considerations have not generally been a determinant of housing choices (there are notable exceptions of course such as proximity to toxic waste sites, etc). When substantive research findings relate the design of urban neighborhoods and the characteristics of their physical or built environments to the health of inhabitants, the urgency and centrality of community design to the health and well-being of urban dwellers is ever greater (Srinivasan, O'Fallon, & Dearry, 2003). We hope to demonstrate in this chapter that as empirical evidence from health research cumulates, the design and redesign of urban environments affects the social behavior of residents as well as their health status. Community design, then, becomes a matter of health and sustainability as well as one of esthetics or personal preference. Indeed, as should become evident, the health consequences of urban design are now a public health priority (O'Donnell, 2003).

HEALTH ISSUES AND DESIGN CONSIDERATIONS FOR
URBAN COMMUNITIES

Five major health issues described below have implications for Urban
communities and, consequently for their design or redesign. These five
health issues have generated significant bodies of empirical evidence
and employ well established research paradigms (1. obesity and inactivity, 2. social connectedness, 3. allostatic load, 4. air quality, and 5.
differential health care access). Each of these five established research
areas is followed by a discussion of the design implications associated
with findings from research. These extrapolations should be viewed as
preliminary until a substantial body of empirical evidence examining
the relationship of built environments to health accumulate The initial
findings in this area of research have enormous potential to contribute
to the promotion of pubic health. As this young science advances new
understandings will emerge regarding built environments and health.

Obesity, Inactivity, and the Built Environment. Estimates suggest that
nearly two thirds of American adults are overweight, and more than 30%
are obese. There are many causes for the rise in obesity, which now
appears to be accelerating to epidemic proportions (Hill, Wyatt, Reed,
& Peters, 2003). Obesity is generally attributed to an excess of sedentary behaviors among adults and children, including television watching
(Hiu, Li, Colditz, Willett, & Manson, 2003) improper diet, including

Principles of New Urbanism

1 Physical definition of streets and public spaces as
   places of shared use.
2 Safety and security but not at expense of accessibility
   and openness.
3 Adequately accommodate automobiles and pedestrians.
4 Streets and squares should be safe, comfortable, and
   interesting to the pedestrian. Properly configured, they
   encourage walking and enable neighbors to know each other
   and protect their communities.
5 Architecture and landscape design should grow from local
   climate, topography, history, and building practice.
6 All buildings should provide their inhabitants with a clear
   sense of location, weather and time.
7 Preservation and renewal of historic builidngs, districts, and
   landscapes affirm the continuity and evolution of urban
   society.

fast foods high in fat. The health consequences of this obesity epidemic
include an increase in type II diabetes, increased risk of heart attack
and stroke, and an increase in cancer risk. Other evidence suggests a
general increase in inflammatory disease associated with obesity
(Malaguti, Castorini, & Lechan, 2004) including an increase in circulat-
ing cytokines. Inflamatory disease may result in an increase in vascular
as well as Alzheimer's related dementia as well. Increasing physical
activity appears to buffer the risk for obesity as well as many diseases.
Although primary care physicians as well as other health professionals
can encourage increases in activity (Eastabrooks, Glasgow, &
Dzewaltowski, 2003), such increases are generally difficult to sustain.
Individual and group interventions to reduce obesity, although initially
effective, are replete with recidivism and reach only a limited number
of individuals. Preventing obesity and encouraging physical activity
through community design is a key element in reducing health disparities in Urban environments.

DESIGNING FOR ACTIVITY: THE NEW URBANIST PERSPECTIVE.

A recent special section of the American Journal of Public Health was
devoted to the interplay between public health and urban planning
(Corburn, 2004). A comparable special issue of the American Journal
of Health Promotion appeared in 2003 (O'Donnell, 2003). Planning
physically active (and, therefore, health promoting) communities
includes redesigning schools, residences, workplaces, public facilities
and spaces, and transportation infrastructure as well as the building
codes at the local and the regional level to encourage physical activity.
New Urbanism addresses the design of urban communities in a manner
consistent with public health priorities.

There are several fundamental principles of New Urbanism, many of
which had origins in Jane Jacobs' (1961) compelling critique of urban
design, that are consistent with the findings from this first research paradigm on obesity and inactivity. Prominent among these New Urbanist
principles is the edict that needed services and public buildings should
be within a five minute walk of the resident. Neighborhoods should be
configured to promote walkability.

A sizeable array of built environment features of neighborhoods consistent with New Urbanism can be reliably measured (Brownson, Chang,

Eyler, Ainsworth, Kirtland, Saelens, & Salis (2004). But only a limited number of these potential perceived neighborhood level design features, such as sidewalks, have been investigated in relationship to physical activity or walking among inhabitants (Addy et al., 2004). We know how to redesign these communities even though we have had difficulty in implementing and evaluating the redesigns. Walkable neighborhoods, according to New Urbanist theory, should promote social contact as well as the monitoring of positive neighborhood interaction.

In order to design walkable neighborhoods, a diverse mix of public buildings, residences, schools, businesses and services, open spaces, parks, transportation possibilities, and recreational facilities must be configured in ways implied by theory. Streets should be interconnected and share pedestrian and vehicular traffic. Innovative New Urban designs include reconfigurable buildings such as loft style residences that combine work and living spaces, small footprint houses with built around public squares, transportation-oriented developments and other mixed use complexes. Areas of historic or cultural significance must be preserved to maintain the character of the neighborhood.

The public health implications of obesity and inactivity for children are particularly alarming. Naturally occurring opportunities for exercise that existed decades ago for youngsters such as walking to school are disappearing. Indeed, as the report by the National Trust for Historic Preservation Report: Why Johnny can't walk to school (Beaumont & Pianca, 2000) illustrates, neighborhood schools are disappearing. The Trust Report notes that many state policies require a minimum of ten acres of land for a school site, plus one acre of land for every 100 students---thus ensuring that children must be bussed to school because residential neighborhoods are not within walking distance of what the report calls "mega-school sprawl" or the construction of school buildings in "remote, middle of nowhere locations that rule out the possibility of anyone's walking to school" (Beaumont & Pianca, 2000, p. 5). Reversing inactivity trends could pay large potential dividends. Even minor changes in diet and activity levels could have significant effects on health and risk status. For example, an increase of even 15 minutes per day of walking or small reductions in eating could affect the energy balance and thereby slow the gradual weight gain in the population (Hill, Wyatt, Reed, & Peters (2003)---or simply adding 2000 steps can

result in weight loss (Larkin, 2003). Apparently, parents and teachers, if not children themselves can agree on ways to combat obesity (e.g., change in available foods in schools, support for physical education programs, etc) (reference RWJ survey). When residents combine with architects, engineers, planners and health experts, thoughtful redesigns are a real possibility. The revision of local and regional master plans and codes is especially crucial to such redesign efforts.

Social Connectedness and Health. The second health issue linked to community design emanates from a fundamental understanding in the social sciences about the relationship of social connectedness to health outcomes (House, Landis, & Umberson, 1988; Adler and Matthews, 1994). Socially isolated individuals are less healthy and more prone to all-cause death rates, including cancer and coronary heart disease (House et al., 1988). The role of social support in immune function has been extensively documented in a field of study called psychoneuroimmunology (Kiecolt-Glaser, McGuire, Robles, & Glaser, R., 2002). Social support has been shown to ameliorate the impact of psychosocial stress on neuroendocrines and in turn their impact on immune function. Social contact with supportive others may actually trigger physiological changes that mediate disease (e.g., a reduction in inflammatory cytokines; or cortisol levels; Malaguti et al., 2004). A significant body of controlled research with animals, for example, suggests that social contact (e.g., cuddling or physical contact) neutralizes the detrimental effects of high fat diets on coronary artery disease (Osipow and Spokane, 1987). As will be obvious from the discussion, social support---including its most focused form (therapeutic intervention) also effectuates healthful changes in behavior and activity, mood and brain activity and bllod chemistry (APA monitor, 2004). Social connectedness mediates disease course, severity, and proneness.

Speculation regarding the underlying mechanisms for the beneficial effects of social connectedness range from strengthening the immune system (Cohen & Herbert, 1996: Kiecolt-Glaser et al., 2002), to improved self care (e.g., diet, exercise), to enhanced mood. Other possible explanations for the buffering effects of social connectedness include reduced time spent ruminating about health concerns, especially in the elderly, and increases in positive health promoting activities such as medication compliance, and improved nutrition. Social connectedness also appears to improve mood and mental health thereby buffering the effects of stress on overall health.

The Domino Park in Little Havana, FL, is one venue where many Hispanic elders connect. Little Havana is also the site of a major NIMH/NIEHS grant study on the relationship between built environments, behavior and health in the elderly over time. The elders in Domino Park generally walk to the park, meet regularly to play dominos, talk, eat at local restaurants and reminisce about their common origins and experiences.

Although we have clear evidence of the health benefits of social support, the most crucial components of social connectedness and the mechanism/s by which social connection improves health are still something of a mystery. What aspects of social connectedness are responsible for its beneficial effects. Is connectedness simply a matter of positive ties, or of a ratio between positive and negative interactions? To what extent is connectedness a function of personality and stable traits, as opposed to the context of the environment in which the individual lives. Much remains to be discovered. Perceived social variables such as other active persons in the neighborhood and trust levels among neighbors, are also correlated with increased levels of walking and overall physical activity (Addy, Wilson, Kirtland, Ainsworth, Sharpe, & Kimsey, 2004).

Balancing social contact and privacy. Social scientists once considered privacy to be the sine qua non of residential and workplace design and related privacy to the concept of territoriality. Crowding was believed to engender interpersonal conflict and frustration and privacy was an essential to individual well-being. We now believe, in contrast, that both privacy and social contact are essential to create a sense of social embeddedness and thereby well-being. Crowding, especially residential density, is still studied and continues to be a factor in behavioral health (Evans, Saegert, & Harris, 2001). Privacy, however, appears to have benefits so long as the privacy is mediated by social support (Evans, Plasane, Lepore, & Martin, 1989). The type of built environment (Evans, Lercher, & Kofler, 2002) appears to affect the sense of privacy. In other words, both privacy and connectedness contribute to a resident's sense of social embeddedness or belonging and a sense of belonging is affected by the structural and architectural features of the built environment. Further, perceptions of privacy and crowding appear

to be heavily dictated by culture as well as gender (Kaya & Weber, 2003). Too much social contact in the absence of privacy results in crowding and potential conflict. Too little contact results in isolation and a loss of the health benefits associated with social connectedness. Personality style may mediate the relationship between social connectedness and health. Roe and Siegelman (1964) for example, demonstrated in anthropological studies that individuals tend to vary in their need for social interaction and could be characterized as either oriented "toward" or "away" from persons. Thus, an individual oriented away from persons and inhabiting a physical environment that does not support social contact might be expected to become isolated to an unhealthy extent both physically and mentally. This individual tendency toward or away from sociability can be reliably measured and we should be conscious in community design that needs for privacy as well as social connectedness may vary across individuals or between cultures. To illustrate the developmental nature of place attractiveness, Clark and Uzzell (2002) found that neighborhoods, schools and town center were attractive to adolescents (presumably for social connectedness), whereas home was not (presumably because privacy was not sought. Similarly, Bures (2003) found that differences in children's neighborhood stability had global effects on self-rated health that persisted into adulthood. The amount of social contact an individual receives may be a function of the number and closeness of relatives and friends, as well as the individual's inclination toward, or need for, social contact. Clearly, in addition, connectedness is affected by activity level and the extent to which the individual is able to seek and obtain social contact. The ideal balance perhaps can be found in homes that provide some privacy and

The New Urbanist Neighborhood Unit

The neighborhood unit is the basic tool for planning livable cities. Its features transcend scale and density: one neighborhood alone in a rural area is a village, several neighborhoods together form a town. Yet in all these cases the neighborhood has five basic features:

1. Identifiable center and edge
2. Limited size (commonly 5 minute walk from center to edge)
3. Mix of uses and housing types
4. Interconnected network of walkable streets
5. Special sites for civic purposes

neighborhoods that provide for social connectedness.

DESIGNING FOR EYES ON THE STREET AND SOCIAL EMBEDEDNESS

A central proposition in New Urbanism is the notion that social monitoring of residential neighborhoods----a phenomenon that New Urbanists call "eyes on the street"--- results in more social control over damaging social conditions such as drug trafficking, crime, and violence. Thus a New Urbanist would value windows and doors facing residential streets, mixed use (residential, business, public use) housing such that activity is continuous across the day and there are few periods when people are not monitoring social behavior. The interface between housing, business and public spaces, then, defines the extent of social monitoring that occurs. New urbanism recognizes the synergy between public and private spaces and seeks to tip the design balance toward connectedness following decades of emphasis on privacy.

The neighborhood unit in New Urban design, is an identifiable, socially cohesive, entity that provides a sense of place and a feeling of social embeddedness. New Urban principles also emphasize soliciting and incorporating community input at multiple points in the design. This essential element in community building contributes to ownership of the resulting built environment and a sense that community needs are being met thus contributing both to a sense of embeddedness as well as eventual reductions in stress reducing conditions (e.g., green spaces). Urban planners and architects are gradually evolving a complex strategy for eliciting individual and community input throughout community design projects. This input is accomplished in a unique forum called a "charrette". A charrette is a forum for the continuous interaction and feedback from a community with redesigners. This highly inclusive and effective venue both solicits input from the community regarding needed design features and elements, and ensures the utility, meaningfulness and appropriateness of the resulting plan.

Allostatic Load and Health Risk. The third health research paradigm affecting community designs investigates the cumulative health consequences of living in stressful urban conditions. Although environments have direct effects on health, there may be several routes by which environmental conditions translate to illness or "get under the skin" (Taylor

and Repetti, 1997). The first route proposed is the differential exposure to chronic stress, or what has been called "allostatic load". A second route is via mental health or mental distress which mediates illness and affects the extent of health promotion behavior of individuals. Both of these routes involve changes in health behavior, and may also compromise the immune competence of individuals. Other physiological changes can be expected to follow (Cohen & Herbert, 1996; Kiecolt-Glaser et al., 2002; Taylor and Repetti, 1997). Generally, life in low socioeconomic status neighborhoods is associated with very high allostatic loads. Although no direct investigations have been conducted, the reduction of allostatic load through community or the facilitation of constructive social behavior is certainly a possibility and as noted below, the methodological tools for such studies are now available.

In a groundbreaking article that ushered in an era of hierarchical linear modeling as a statistical analysis technique, Sampson, Raudenbush and Earls (1997) documented the social consequences of living in distressed neighborhood (i.e., increased allostatic load). Sampson et al. (1997) examined the notion that the social and environmental characteristics of neighborhoods account for increases in violent crime, independent of the demographic characteristics of the inhabitants. Sampson et al. found that the "collective efficacy" among inhabitants in a neighborhood substantially mediated the relationship between demographics and violent crime. In other words, although socioeconomic status (SES) was related to crime, collective efficacy was a predictor of crime independent of SES. Other studies confirm the relationship of perceptions of the physical environment of street blocks and crime and disorder (Perkins, Meeks, & Taylor, 1992: Taylor, Shumaker, & Gottfredson, 1985) as well as the buffering effects of social ties (Ross & Jang, 2000). Thus allostatic load can presumably be lessened by supportive social behavior. Several New Urbanist principles (e.g., safe, comfortable well configured streets and squares, sense of place, esthetics and preservation of historic districts, etc) may also lessen allostatic load.

In addition to these general New Urban Design principles, consistent with our culture-centered emphasis, cultural markers can be embedded as design elements, contributing to a sense of place, cultural familiarity and identity thus lessening allostatic load. Increasingly, ethnic enclaves are viewed as an alternative to assimilation for immigrant subgroups.

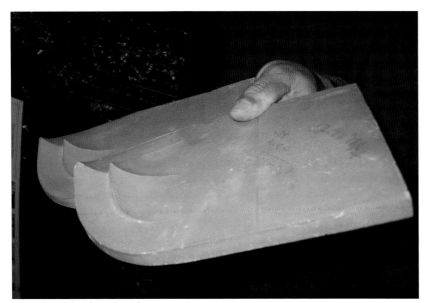

Figure 1   Fishscale roofing tiles.

Figure 2   Lotus towers and roof lines.

Such enclaves permit the individual to remain connected to a culture of origin and to create a "sense of place" compatible with their self-identity (Brown, Perkins, & Brown, 2003; Mazumdar, Mazumdar, Docuyanan, & McLaughlin, 2000). A culturally compatible neighborhood strengthens positive bonds between the individual and the physical and social environment. Embedding cultural markers from representative community groups requires both identifying those subgroups and then extracting cultural symbols that might be incorporated in building designs.

A recent design charrette in San Jose California conducted by the Knight Fellows in Community Building serves as a model for embedding cultural elements in community redesign. One of two dominant representative populations in San Jose's Evergreen-Eastridge area, Vietnamese cultural elements were readily identifiable, the second dominant group, Mexican-American, also has identifiable cultural icons and symbols. Both groups were extensively representing during the charrette process.

Fish scale roofing tiles characteristic of Vietnamese designs are illustrated in Figure 1 as well as Lotus towers and characteristic rooflines depicted in Figure 2.

As can be readily seen in Figure 4 several of these design elements were integrated into an integrative design of fourplex residential units for the Evergreen Eastridge Area (drawing by Professor Jaime Correa, University of Miami) that would permit extended families to maintain both privacy and extended family ties by living in the same building but in separate building units (see Figure 4).

It is well worth noting that several of the cultural design elements of Vietnamese and Mexican-American culture overlap---both employ common courtyards and both use natural clay tiles. Therefore, these two design elements were embedded in the ingenious fourplex drawing by Professor Correa. We now proceed to the final two health issues in community design, air quality and differential access to health care.

Air Quality and Health. Among the environmental contaminants that have direct health effects, particulate matter in the air, and lead in paints are two of the most insidious. Asthma, lung disorders (e.g. emphysema, lung cancer) are exacerbated by particulate matter in the air, in particular ammonium nitrate (Fairley, 1999). There is a continued association between air pollutants and mortality in spite of air quality standards (Fairley, 1999). This association is especially consequential for the health of children with regard to post neonatal mortality, asthma hospitalizations, emergency department visits, school absences and lower birth weights with estimated health costs in the billions of dollars (Wong, Gohlke, Griffith, Farrow, & Faustman, 2004). Comparable findings in developing countries have prompted the World Health Organization to press for greater integration between health and environmental concerns (Suter, 2004) and to publish an atlas illustrating the impact of the environment on children's health (Gordon, Mackay, & Rehfuess, 2004). The sheer number of global environmental issues affecting children is enormous and each issue has significant health outcomes. These environmental concerns affecting children's health include poverty, clean water, sanitation, arsenic indoor smoke,

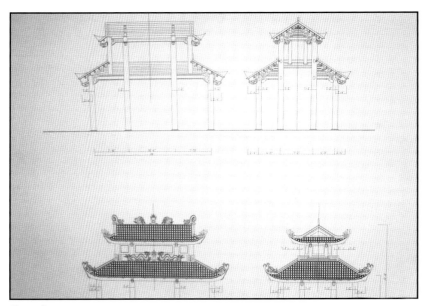

Figure 3

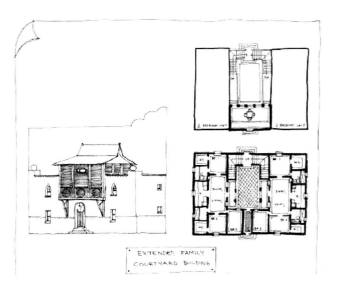

Figure 4   Culturally sensitive fourplex design. J. Correa, 2002

air pollution, child labor and injuries, lead and other contaminants, safe food supplies and safe schools. The issue most relevant to community design, however, is the nitrogen oxides that result from gases generated by power plants, factories, and vehicular traffic (Gordon et al., 2004). The health effects on children---and adults and elders include pneumonia and lower respiratory infections, asthma, and low birth weight.

Air Pollution is particularly relevant to urban design. Transportation data in the US clearly show the increase in vehicular traffic (mostly trucks) that can be attributed in part to the design and construction of vehicle-dependent communities. Increasing walkability, decreasing vehicular volume and speed (traffic calming) and an increase in transit-oriented community design are fundamental principles of New Urban theory, and can all contribute to reduced concentrations of particulate matter in the air. We now move on to the fifth health issue relevant to the design of healthy communities---differential health care access.

Differential Health Care Access and Utilization. A large body of literature verifies the underutilization of health and mental health services by certain social groups (thus the term "underserved"). This differential access is a significant factor in health disparity (Srinivasan et al., 2003). The scope of underutilization is pervasive with, for example, early disparities in preschool immunizations (Chu, Barker, & Smith, 2004) between Black and White children widening by as much as 1% per year (Chu et al., 2004). Similar findings pertain to oral and dental health service utilization (Formicola, et al., 2004), preventative health services (Banks-Wallace, Enyart, & Johnson 2004), and clinical trials research (Murthy, Krumholz, & Gross, 2004). Underutilization by minority and low SES subgroups is a significant contributor to health disparities.

Consider why certain subgroups might not utilize health services even when they are available. The reasons may be several. An individual may not recognize the need for medical care, or, may be uninsured and concerned about ability to pay. An individual may be reluctant to seek help for reasons of privacy or cultural appropriateness. Clearly, however, the availability of routine health care services within walking distance of underserved residents promotes access to healthcare. Neighborhood clinics, doctors offices, and preventative services interspersed in a neighborhood with good diversity of use (a mix of commercial, residential and institutional buildings; Jacobs, 1961), according to New Urban Theory, should promote access to needed social and healthcare services. Zoning laws, then, must permit mixed use, and incentives may need to exist to attract health professionals to low SES urban neighborhoods. A Research and Theory-Building Agenda in Built Environments, Behavior and Health

As Taylor, Repetti, & Seeman ably noted (1997), little research has examined the relationship of community characteristics to mental health, and there is even less emphasis on community characteristics and physical health. We add, that there are very few studies on built environment characteristics and health, especially longitudinal studies. Although the situation is somewhat better in 2004 than it was ten years ago, the basic propositions that Taylor et al. (1997) detailed remain largely unexamined. As Taylor et al. (1997) observed, progress has been made in identifying the individual precursors of chronic illness, but it remains clear that "these predictors are nested within geographic, developmental, occupational, and social environments". Such nested relationships have been difficult to analyze but can now be understood using Hierarchical Linear Modeling (HLM; Bryk & Raudenbush, 2002). HLM permits the analysis of relationships that are nested within circumscribed geographic units (e.g., neighborhoods, residential blocks, schools, and communities) which can be identified using geomapping. These statistical advances permit the empirical test of social ecology models such as Bronfenbrenner (1979) in powerful ways impossible until now. As a result, the number, range, and scope of investigations relating the built environments to health when mediated by social behavior are expanding at a very rapid pace.

We have discussed five prominent health issues (obesity, inactivity and health; social connectedness and health, allostatic load and health risk, air quality and health, differential health care access and utilization). We have also presented some of the design implications for built environments, behavior and health that derive from these five health research paradigms. Many more health outcomes will likely be related to environmental precursors as this area of research matures. The interdisciplinary, cross-cultural, multi-methodological nature of these new studies makes them among the most intriguing and potentially practical in the applied sciences. The role of the built environment in health disparities, then, is a vigorous and growing science. What are the central questions/issues that this new science should address?

A RESEARCH AGENDA ON BUILT ENVIRONMENTS BEHAVIOR AND HEALTH

We pose the following research and theory questions as a research agenda for the emerging science of built environments, behavior and health:

1. Valid and reliable objective measures of the specific characteristics of the built environment are needed. Most recent studies rely upon subjective reactions to the built environment, or gross measures of neighborhood characteristics when environmental variables are included for study. This problem is not a new one in the social and behavioral sciences and while some initial measures are becoming available, validity and reliability evidence have been slow in coming.

2. Once valid and reliable measures are available we will be in a better position to examine which aspects of built environments have the greatest impact on behavior and health? Are those characteristics hypothesized by New Urbanism (e.g., walkable streets, more porches and windows on the street, mixed building use, traffic calming, etc) related to health?

3. What are the mediators, underlying mechanisms by which these built environment characteristics exert their influence? Stated another way, what is it, specifically about neighborhood, work, and educational environments that affects health? Conceivably there may protective as well as toxic qualities that interact to produce health outcomes.

4. Do the effects of built environments on health and mental health vary with age in either a linear, or curvelinear manner. For example if some environments are better for children and elders than adults at midlife the result may be different models at different developmental stages (e.g., adolescence, adulthood, late adulthood) or a comprehensive model that incorporates age or stage of life when examining relationships between the built environment and health..

5. How does the social behavior of inhabitants mediate the effects of built environments upon health? Which aspects of social support are most salutary and why? Are there cultural differences in how social support mediates behavior and health or is this phenomenon universal.

6. What extent of changes in built environments is necessary to result in an improvement in the mental and physical health of inhabitants? Will such changes result in improved health status.

7. What are the economic consequences of the built environment characteristics and design? What are the costs of changes in the built environment in relation to benefits achieved? A good example here is the potential financial and social costs of removing elders from their natural environments because those environments do not provide needed support.

8. Can we successfully integrate findings and methods from other disciplines to provide a more comprehensive model of the built environment behavior and health?

The West Grove project is a laboratory for the study of human behavior and health in the physical environment. Another example of such a laboratory exists in Little Havana, Fl in which more specific built environment measures are being developed and validated with Hispanic Elders (Szapocznik et al., in preparation). Others exist in the US and around the world, funded by NIEHS, The Robert Wood Johnson Foundation, and the CDC, that are beginning to produce solid empirical findings. The future of this emerging science of built environments behavior and health, as a result, looks most promising.

This chapter was supported in part by grants from the Robert Wood Johnson Foundation (Grant No. 037377, a joint grant from the National Institute of Mental Health, the National Institute of Environmental Health Sciences (Grant No. MH063709) to José Szapocznik Ph.D. (PI) and a John S. and James L. Knight Foundation grant to Elizabeth Plater Zyberk.

REFERENCES

Addy, C. L., Wilson, D. K., Kirtland, K. A., Ainsworth, B. E., Sharpe, P., & Kimsey, D. (2004). Associations of perceived social and physical environmental supports with physical activity and walking. American Journal of Public Health, 94, 440 – 443.

Adler, N., & Matthews, K. (1994). Health psychology: Why do some people get sick and some stay well? Annual Review of Psychology, 45, 229 – 259.

Banks-Wallace, J., Enyart, J., & Johnson, C. (2004). Recruitment and entrance of participants into a physical activity intervention for hypertensive African American Women. Advances in Nursing Science, 27, 102 – 116.

Beaumont, C. E., & Pianca, E. G. (2000). Historic neighborhood schools in the age of sprawl: Why Johnny can't walk to school. Washington, DC: National Trust for Historic Preservation.

Bronfenbrenner, U. (1979). The ecology of human development. Cambridge, MA: Harvard University Press.

Bryk, A. S., & Raudenbush, S. W. (2002). Hierarchical linear models: Application and data analysis methods. (2nd ed.) Newbury Park, CA: Sage.

Brown, B., Perkins, D. D., & Brown, G. (2003). Place attachment in a revitalizing neighborhood: Individual and block level of analysis. Journal of Environmental Psychology, 23, 259 – 271.

Brownson, R. C., Chang, J. J., Eyler, A. A., Ainsworth, B. E., Kirtland, K. A., Saelens, B. E., & Sallis, J. F. (2004). Measuring the environment for friendliness toward physical activity: A comparison of the reliability of 3 questionnaires. American Journal of Public Health, 94, 473 – 483.

Bures, R. M. (2003). Childhood residential stability and health at midlife. American Journal of Public Health, 93, 1144 – 1151.

Chu, S. Y., Barker, L. E., & Smith, P. J. (2004). Racial/ethnic disparities in preschool immunizations: United States, 1996-2001. American Journal of Public Health, 94, 973 – 977.

Clark, C., & Uzzell, D. L. (2002). The affordances of the home, neighbourhood, school and town centre for adolescents. Journal of

Environmental Psychology, 22, 95 – 108.

Cohen, S., & Herbert, T. B. (1996). Health psychology: Psychological factors and physical disease from the perspective of human psychoneuroimmunology. Annual Review of Psychology, 47, 113 – 142.

Congress of the New Urbanism (2000). Charter of the New Urbanism. New York: McGraw Hill or http://www.cnu.org.

Corburn, J. (2004). Confronting the challenges in reconnecting urban planning and public health. American Journal of Public Health, 94, 541 – 545.

Duany, A., & Plater-Zyberk, E. (1992). The second coming of the small American Town. Wilson Quarterly, 16, 19 – 48.

Eastabrooks, P. A., Glasgow, R. E., Dzewaltowski, D. A. (2003). Physical activity promotion through primary care. JAMA, 289, 2913 – 2916.

Evans, G. W., Lercher, P., & Kofler, W. W. (2002). Crowding and children's mental health: the role of house type. Journal of Environmental Psychology, 22, 221 – 231.

Evans, G. W., Palsane, M. N., Lepore, S. L., & Martin, J. (1989). Residential density and psychological health: The mediating effects of social support. Journal of Personality and Social Psychology, 57, 994 – 999.

Evans, G. W., Saegert, S., & Harris, R. (2001). Residential density and psychological   health among children in low income families. Environment and Behavior, 33, 165 – 180.

Fairley, D. (1999). Daily mortality and air pollution in Santa Clara County California: 1989-1996. Environmental Health Perspectives, 107, 637 – 648.

Formicola, A. J., Ro, M.,, Marshall, S., Derksen, D., Powell, W., Hartsock, L., & Treadwell, H.M. (2004). Strengthening the oral healoth safety net: Delivery models that improve access to oral health care for uninsures and underserved populations. American Journal of Public Health, 94, 702 – 704.

Gordon, B., Mackay, R., & Rehfuess, E. (2004). Inheriting the world: The atlas of children's health and the environment. Geneva: World Health Organization.

Hill, J. O., Wyatt, H. R., Reed, G. W., & Peters, J. C. (2003). Obesity and the environment: Where do we go from here? Science, 299, 853-856.

Hiu, F. B., Li, T. Y., Colditz, G. A., Willett, W. C., & Manson, J. E. (2003). Television watching and other sedentary behaviors in relation to risk of obesity and type 2 diabetes mellitus in women. JAMA, vol 289, pp. 1785- 1792.

House, J. S., Landis, K. R., & Umberson, D. (1988). Social relationships and health. Science, 241, 540 – 54.

Jacobs, J. (1961). The death and life of great American cities. New York: Vintage.

Ji, L., Peng, K., & Nisbett, R. E. (2000). Culture, control, and perception of relationships in the environment. Journal of Personality & Social Psychology, 78, 943 – 955.

Kaya, N., & Weber, M. J. (2003). Cross-cultural differences in the perceptions of crowding and privacy regulation: American and Turkish students. Journal of Environmental Psychology, 23, 301 – 309.

Kiecolt-Glaser, J., McGuire, L., Robles, T. F., & Glaser, R. (2002). Emotions, morbidity and mortality: New perspectives from psychoneuroimmunology. Annual Review   of Psychology, 53, 83 – 107.

Larkin, M. (2003). Can cities be designed to fight obesity? Urban planners and health experts work to get people up and about. Lancet, 362, 1046 – 1047.

Lavizzo-Mourey, R., & McGinnis, M. (2003). Making the case for active living communities. American Journal of Public Health, 93, 1386 – 1390.

Malaguti, T. R., Castorina, R., Roti, E., & Lechan, R. M. (2004). New paradigms in neuroendocrinology: Relationships between obesity, sytemmatic inflammation and the neuroendocrine system. Journal of Endocrinological Investigation, 27, 182 – 186.

Mazumdar, S., Mazumdar, S., Docuyanan, F., & McLaughlin, C. M. (2000). Creating a sense of place: The Vietnamese-Americans and Little Saigon. Journal of Environmental Psychology, 20, 319 – 333.

Murthy, V. H., Krumholz, H. M., & Gross, C. P. (2004). Participation in cancer clinical trials: Race-, sex-, and age-based disparities. JAMA, 291, 2720 -2726.

O'Donnell, M. P. (2003). Editor's notes. American Journal of Health Promotion, 18, iv –v.

Orleans, C. T., Kraft, K. M., Marx, J. F., & McGinnis, M. J. (2003). Why are some neighborhoods active and others not? Charting a new course for research on the policy and environmental determinants of physical activity. Annals of Behavioral Medicine, 25, 77 – 79.

Osipow, S. H., & Spokane, A. R. (1987). Manual for Measures of Occupational Stress, Strain, and Coping. Odessa, FL: Psychological Assessment Resources (PAR).

Perkins, D. D., Meeks, J. W., & Taylor, R. B. (1992). The physical environment of street blocks and resident perceptions of crime and disorder: Implications for theory and measurement. Journal of Environmental Psychology, 12, 21 – 34.

Pick, S., Poortinga, Y. H., & Givaudan, M. (2003). Integrating intervention theory and strategy in culture-sensitive health promotion programs. Professional Psychology: Research and practice, 34, 422 – 429.

Roe, A., & Siegelman, M. (1964). The origins of interests. APGA Inquiry Series, NO. 1. Washington, D. C.: American Personnel and Guidance Association.

Ross, C. E., & Jang, S. J. (2000). Neighborhood disorder, fear and mistrust: The buffering role of social ties with neighbors. American Journal of Community Psychology, 28, 401 – 421.

Sampson, R. J., Raudenbush, S. W., & Earls, F. (1997). Neighborhoods and violent crime: A multilevel study of collective efficacy. Science, 277, 918 – 924.

Sen, A. (2000). Development as freedom. Anchor.

Shepard, R. (2002). The affordable house in Coconut Grove (pp. 75 – 81). In S. Quraeshi (Ed.). The living traditions of Coconut Grove. Miami, FL. University of Miami School of Architecture.

Spokane, A. R., Fouad, N. A., & Swanson, J. L (2002). Culture-centered career intervention. Journal of Vocational Behavior, Srinivasan, S., O'Fallon, L. R., & Dearry, A. (2003). Creating healthy communities, healthy homes, healthy people: Initiating a research agenda on the built environment and public health. American Journal of Public Health, 93, 1446.

Szapocznik, J., & Kurtines, W. M. (1993). Family psychology and cultural diversity: Opportunities for theory, research, and application. American Psychologist, 48, 400 – 407.

Szapocznik, J., Lombard, J., Martinez, F, Mason, C., Gorman-Smith, D, Plater-Zyberk, L. Brown, S., & Spokane, A. R. (2004). New Urbanism's built environment theory predicts school outcomes. (submitted to American Journal of Public Health).

Suter, G. W. 2nd. (2004). Bottom-up and top-down integration of human and ecological risk assessment. Journal of Toxilogical and Environmental Health, 67, 779 – 790.

Taylor, R. B., Sumaker, S. A.,M & Gottfredson, S. D. (1985). Neighborhood-level links between physical features and local sentiments deterioration, fear of crime, and confidence. Journal of Architectural Planning Research. 2, 261 – 275.

Taylor & Repetti (1997). Annual Review of Psychology.

Wong, E. Y., Gohlke, J., Griffith, W. C., Farrow, S., & Faustman, E. M. (2004). Assessing the health benefits of air pollution roduction for children. Environmental Health Perspectives, 112, 226 – 232.

The Tie That Binds
The Role of the Law School Clinic in Community Building

Anthony Alfieri
University of Miami School of Law

Kelley Spencer
University of Miami School of Law
Community Economic Development and Design Clinic

AN INTRODUCTORY NOTE

As revisions to the following essay were underway, the Community Economic Development and Design ("CEDAD") clinic at the University of Miami School of Law called an emergency meeting. Twenty low-income tenants living in the West Coconut Grove had phoned the clinic after receiving a surprising eviction notice. Their landlord informed them that their building had been sold and that they had fifteen days to evacuate. The tenants were on an informal month-to-month lease and the short notice was all that was required by law. A few days prior, during a landlord-tenant law presentation given by CEDAD to residents of the West Grove, a group of tenants asked about their rights in light of a recent rent increase that had nearly quadrupled their present rate. Again, the increase was lawful. Due to the policy shift by the Department of Housing and Urban Development that favors mixed-use development and a public housing waitlist that numbers more than 64,000 persons, there are no housing options for the tenants in their neighborhood.

With the holidays fast approaching, we gathered that afternoon to discuss the options and the mood was strikingly somber. After a semester of studying the plight of low-income neighborhoods like the West Grove and working to fight against the forces pushing black residents of the West Grove from their neighborhood, we were suddenly living gentrification; that word had suddenly become real. As our practice group leader, Anthony V. Alfieri, Law Professor at the University of Miami School of Law, related to us that he faced the same formidable situation over twenty years ago as a poverty lawyer in New York City, the full com-

plexity of the problems faced by low-income neighborhoods was evident. "This is what happens," Alfieri told the group. And while the frustration of not being able to uncover a legal recourse for these mothers and their children was paralyzing, there was something very positive to be found in that moment. There were tenants of an impoverished neighborhood who, after assessing their situation, knew that a joint-venture partnership at the University of Miami that worked in their neighborhood could help them. There were students, humbled by the reality of their work, who plotted a course of action using the language and theory behind the client-centered approach to community development lawyering. And there was a community that stood to gain from lessons learned by the law school clinic, CEDAD.

The following essay seeks to highlight those lessons learned by the student, the resident, and the community through the exploration of CEDAD. The section on community economic development and problem-solving examines the territory of development in light of the urban crisis and a new approach to solving problems in low-income neighborhoods. The following section makes a case for pairing clinical education with the process of community building. The focus of that section is on what each actor learns so that the overarching purpose of interdisciplinary joint-venture partnerships may be understood: that the qualities of this approach to problem-solving are the very qualities that help the process to overcome historic obstacles, allowing the solution, whatever it may be, to take hold in the neighborhoods and to grow organically from there, empowering as it goes.

COMMUNITY ECONOMIC DEVELOPMENT PROBLEM-SOLVING

Economic development—in recent years the phrase has become a catch-all slogan for a number of projects and agendas, conjuring varied notions of what palpable progress is or ought to be. The phrase is used to justify the budgetary spending of millions of dollars by municipal governments to enhance the aesthetic "quality" of cities. It is employed by the State Department in order to push neo-liberal economic policies into the international sphere. Economic development is the subject of countless Community Development Corporations and grassroots organizations. But what that phrase means to residents of an impoverished community, like the West Coconut Grove, in Miami, ranked just a few years ago as the most impoverished city in America [1],

176

is an entirely different issue.

Take, for example, the view of a mother of three interviewed by Professor Tony Alfieri, while working in a neighborhood legal aid office: "They shut off my lights in November, when my kids' food stamps were first reduced. It was around Thanksgiving. I was twenty-four hours without gas and electric. They shut it off because I couldn't pay the gas and electric bill. I had taken the money from my public assistance check to buy food for that month for me and my kids.." [2]

The victim of state-imposed food stamp reduction, this mother was forced to make the decision between food and electricity. Her perception of economic development? State-sanctioned poverty. Down the street from her lives an old man who has spent his life in a low-income neighborhood. He is part of the informal social network that residents of low-income neighborhoods survive on and his sense of identity is tied to that place. He looks across the yard to a brown field that was recently sold by the city to an out-of-state private development firm. The plan is to build condos for a new transient crowd with subsidies from the city government that are generated by increasing property taxes in the area. The old man has no choice—taxes are too high and rent is too expensive. Uprooted, he must leave the neighborhood and find another landlord in another locale that isn't threatened yet by marketability. Most likely, he will find himself in a neighborhood underneath Interstate 95, void of the networks that he spent a lifetime developing in order to make life more bearable. His perception of economic development? State-sponsored gentrification and the de facto construction of visible poverty lines.

When economics ceases to be the science of choice and instead turns into making choices in order to survive, all notions of development are failing. The residents of low-income, non-white, and immigrant neighborhoods have been telling their stories for some time, and lawyers and activists have been retelling those stories. Nonetheless, frustration and confusion permeate the environment in blighted neighborhoods. Luce Professor in Family and Community at the University of Miami School of Architecture's Center for Urban and Community Design, Samina Quraeshi, explains, "There is confusion about the needs that government agencies perceive, or organize themselves to deliver. Often the conditions in these neighborhoods are generalized into a 'one-size fits

all approach' that ignores the special circumstances surrounding each human problem." [3]

This is the crisis of problem-solving in the urban landscape—gaps between marginalized sectors of society and their respective local, state, and federal governments. The status quo, hierarchical top-bottom or trickle down methodology of problem-solving has not been responsive to need; nor has the Welfare State been an effective, accountable response. As Ira Harkavy, Director for the Center for Community Partnerships at the University of Pennsylvania, testified before a Senate committee, "[w]e still do not know how to create and sustain the face-to-face, caring and responsible community...Given a world of intense and intensifying global competition and of continuous and increasingly rapid change, and given the human suffering found in our deteriorating urban areas, the need to solve the [problem] has never been more pressing." [4]

While we continue to search for that responsible community, a rethinking of the problem-solving process has taken hold in many law schools that are dedicated to the community building process. Many believe that solutions to reoccurring problems in community development can be found within the new approach to problem-solving. Law Professor and clinical education trailblazer, Gerald P. Lopez, supervisor of the Community Economic Development Clinic at the New York University Law School, notes:

"Constituencies report informally that, across the nation, the most stubborn obstacles to effective problem solving emanate from the all-too-familiar failure of all-too-many public and private problem solvers to embrace client communities as crucial collaborators...and to cultivate the willingness to challenge over and over whatever we happen to create, no matter how successful and comfortable the regime." [5]

In response to these failures, community economic development clinics, informed by what Lopez calls the "rebellious vision," have realigned their efforts to put community knowledge at the center of their projects. The "rebellious vision," Lopez writes, "[is] in defiance of the long-reigning theory of public and private problem-solving, this vision embraces...the belief that all (from the most subordinated to the most privileged) can and should shape how we might better cope and thrive." [6] As applied to the community economic development clinic, the vision translates as the serious engagement of residents in the initiative building and policy making processes. The residents need to understand where it is that they stand vis-à-vis the government's development agenda and make informed decisions based on their rights as citizens of a democracy, regardless of race, gender, or class. The system of law and policy-making process needs to expand in order to incorporate all claims, needs, and wants. Community economic development clinics provide a space for employing the techniques necessary to achieve that end.

CLINICAL EDUCATION FOR COMMUNITY BUILDING

A perennial complaint made by lawyers is the lack of preparation they received as law students for the actual practice of law. Lawyers, students, and professors alike decry the traditional legal education as devoid of any practical training for growing fields of transactional and litigation work. Lawyers, whether employed by the government, legal services, non-profits, or private firms, are increasingly working within the field of economic development with little training on which to draw. At the same time, residents of low-income neighborhoods decry the system as devoid of any genuine solutions or dedicated problem-solvers, lamenting the vicious cycles of poverty, marginalization, and deterioration.

The community economic development clinic has followed suit by providing a space for the economic development discourse and the implementation of projects with an eye towards community empowerment, once again filling the gap between tradition and the new reality. [7] What used to be the all white, male, public interest group's law reform clinic that grew out of the Great Society and the anti-movements of the 1960s now looks more like CEDAD. Borne of the enterprise of University of Miami School of Architecture Professors Samina Quraeshi

and Richard Shepard and School of Law Professor Anthony Alfieri, CEDAD is currently engaging students from every type of background and career aspiration. The birth of the clinic has been part of what legal scholar John Dubin refers to as a "resurgence in focus on...social justice dimensions;" explaining that, "the emergence of critical lawyering theory, theoretics of practice scholarship and the influence of other postmodernist critical schools of legal thought have heightened the academy's interest in...transforming the social consciousness...by deconstructing power and privilege in law." [8]

While most economic development clinics begin by taking inventory of the need in targeted city neighborhoods, CEDAD was given the unique advantage of capitalizing on the work of the University of Miami Initiative for Urban and Social Ecology (INUSE) and the Center for Urban and Community Design (CUCD). These groups focused on the physically and socially deteriorating West Coconut Grove neighborhood, a close neighbor of the University, yet far from the same status that the University's elite address enjoys. Such conspicuous inequities often prompt universities to develop service projects; yet CUCD was going beyond those traditional public service projects by breaking down the borders between disciplines that have historically impeded the potential for an aggregate impact. Recognizing the intersection of law and design at every corner, CUCD looked to the Center for Ethics and Public Service at the School of Law as a necessary collaborator and CEDAD was chartered as a legal mechanism to support community building.

The first collaborative projects between the two schools had the double objective of research and action. Ranging from the production of small business workshops that complimented CUCD's commercial corridor recommendations to the community legal rights education project focused primarily on landlord-tenant law, each project was accompanied by CEDAD's founding clinical research protocols. These protocols included: A study of the history of the West Coconut Grove, the interdisciplinary literature of small business counseling and economic development training, and the curricular structure of small business and economic development clinics at U.S. law schools. [9] To compliment the efforts aimed at local business ownership was the creation of the community land trust designed to protect the neighborhood from the forces of gentrification. Both projects enlisted the work of architecture students and law students jointly.

Building on the fundamental partnerships and the blanket of research established by the first interns, numbering only three, CEDAD has blossomed over the years, extending its membership as well as its breadth of expertise and potential impact. Projects dealing with landlord-tenant law have increased awareness of tenants in the neighborhood, empowering residents to employ self-help advocacy while more business-oriented law students have conducted training sessions on corporate compliance for non-profit organizations rooted in low-income neighborhoods.

CEDAD recently achieved full live-client clinical status, which permits direct representation of low-income clients in administrative, legal, and legislative tribunals by students under the supervision of a lawyer who has passed the Florida bar, and functions as a workshop divided into a practicum and a seminar. The practicum is dedicated to the fieldwork ranging from furthering the interests of the community land trust in West Coconut Grove to blowing the whistle on the local government's inequitable practices in allocation of resources and services in public housing discrimination in the greater Miami-Dade County. The seminar is an in-depth survey of scholarship dedicated to the subject area of live client law school clinics and fosters an understanding of the issues particular to rebellious lawyering. In the practicum, the students gain the practical experience of working as a community development lawyer; while in the seminar they are provided the opportunity to place that experience within a theoretical context.

The clinic's interdisciplinary, multidimensional approach to problem-solving mixes theory and practice. While the theoretics of poverty law and rebellious lawyering have been criticized by those who believe the field is unpredictable in practice, a "theoretical analysis of practice is commanded by the historical failure of poverty law traditions to countenance the values and to design effective methods of client and other community empowerment, and moreover, by the import of critical theory in the domains of power, gender, and race." [10] The law school clinic, then, as a precursor to the actual practice of law, is the perfect forum for such an undertaking.

WHAT THE STUDENT LEARNS

More often than not, clinic workshops are the only courses on the registrar's list that treat the interplay between the law and about one-quarter of this nation's total population as legitimate subject matter. Given that the biased tradition of legal education has neglected this growing and all important field of law, clinics are one of the few avenues whereby a law student can confidently enter into what, in the past, has been the grey area of public interest law. On the practical side, clinics are ensuring the professional competency of law students by allowing them to engage in the actual practice with supervision and providing a space for reflection on best, and worst, practices. [11]

Perhaps one of the most important aspects of clinical education is the critical analysis of the attorney-client relationship. The traditional, and what rebellious lawyers call paternalistic, approach to counseling, whereby the lawyer dominates the client's voice, is not a sufficiently effective model for problem-solving in low-income neighborhoods. That the client knows more than the lawyer is a counter-intuitive notion to most steeped in American legal culture. Nevertheless, central to the rebellious vision of problem-solving is the inversion of the status quo relationship between the subordinated and the dominated, between the third and the first world, between the periphery and the center. Asymmetries of information have plagued the sociolegal world as evidenced by the attorney-client relationship in the practice of progressive lawyering. Many times the interaction between a progressive lawyer and the subordinated client undermines the autonomy of the client— a power-relation that is repugnant to liberal theory. Many times this interaction undercuts the value of the client's day-to-day problem-solving skills in environments with scarce resources—a vital element of the client's livelihood. The client can be undermined in ways as subtle as the lawyer's "storytelling" where she transforms a client's original narrative is into another representative, yet false, form. The undermining can be as overt as a lawyer's decision to go against the wishes of the client in order to get to an end that is in the lawyer's mind, the appropriate end. Anthony Alfieri explains, in review of Lopez, his prescription:

To realign lawyer-client authority, Lopez recommends reversing the "marginalization" of clients' "local knowledge." Reversal hinges on

Photo courtesy of CEDAD

believing clients to be "capable" moral agents equipped "with a will to fight, and with considerable experience in resisting and occasionally reversing subordinated status." Treating clients as capable fighters in the struggle against subordination affirms a practical expertise that compliments lawyers' knowledge. The inability of lawyers and clients to uncover this complementary potential is in part a function of unequal institutional roles and relations. [12]

Students learn that "contrary to the conventional myth of dependency, a poor client is an autonomous subject capable of both accommodating and resisting the commands of sociolegal actors." [13] To deconstruct this myth and engage the client as collaborator, Anthony Alfieri explains that lawyers and clinic students must engage in the practice of bicultural and bilingual translation:

This method of translation, Lopez explains, "moves in two directions, creating both a meaning for the legal culture out of the situations that people are living and a meaning for people's practices out of the legal culture." Meaning derives from understanding "the client's experience of the situation" given her own "categories and characterizations of daily living. For Lopez, getting a "feel" for the client's situation—what she "thinks, feels, needs, and desires"—is pivotal. By getting the feel of a "client's social (not just legal) situation," lawyers may be able to acquire fluency in discourses of difference and to construct client identity in terms of problem-solving and managerial competence. [14]

The development of the client-centered approach to counseling and advocacy, designed to foster client decision-making and enhance the likelihood that decisions are truly the clients, has been widely received by all attorneys practicing in the field and continues to be enhanced by clinicians. [15] Through this approach, students are taught to avoid the "interpersonal domination of clients by lawyers; the disempowerment that accompanies reliance on litigation-based dispute resolution or its equivalent; and the inefficacy of intrasystemic remedies to achieve meaningful change in the lives of poor clients." [16] The client-centered model engenders a mutually beneficial relationship by allowing for a bilateral transaction of ideas and values. This approach, in turn, builds trust and familiarity into the attorney-client relationship, overcoming the most stubborn obstacle in representing the underrepresented.

Another key aspect of the educational process is preparing the student for dealing with the volatile and fragmented environments that progressive lawyers often encounter in their daily practice. There is no fluid concept of poverty law, no real ABA standards for the representation of indigent clients. In a line of work that is founded by the concepts of organization and order, rebellious lawyering in low-income neighborhoods can surprise even the most suspecting of law clinic students. Having to acclimate to an environment that functions outside of the formal system and somehow bring those issues into line with the formal legal system, and to do all of this without undermining the client's collaborative force, is a daunting task. To that end, the field projects—taking the students into the fragmented neighborhoods, understaffed Legal Services offices, and bureaucratic municipal buildings— force the students to experience first hand just how difficult collaboration is—especially when the advocates themselves don't have the answers to the problems for which they are encouraging collaboration. For this reason, the focus must always be on informing and improving the problem-solving process itself while collaborating with the residents. Quickly, students learn to heed the advice of Lopez, that in this realm of practice, we must work "always understanding [that] we will often fall flat on our faces, and certainly never figure 'it' all out." [17]

WHAT THE RESIDENT LEARNS

In response to the marginalization and inadequate representation of the poor, the ABA Comprehensive Legal Needs Study revealed that in low-income households only three of every ten legal problems are brought into the legal system [18], reminding us of. theories such as legal scholar Marc Galanter's classic piece where he explains the powerful influence of class on the legal system through a dichotomy of repeat players, the "haves" and one-shot players, the "have nots." [19] CEDAD promulgates the rebellious vision of problem-solving as the first step in attaining equality of outcomes before the law. As employed by CEDAD, this problem-solving process offers a model for the integration of the collaborative force and pool of knowledge that have been underutilized through years of inefficient development endeavors. The qualities of the model create a bilateral exchange of information so that the resident partaking in the process is learning from the counselor and, more importantly, from her own voice.

The service projects offer the resident a substantive education on issues relevant to community building. The generation of a locally-owned commercial infrastructure is a dominant theme in the story of economic development. To this end, interested residents partake in small business start-up and credit counseling workshops that are tailored to meet the needs of developing businesses in areas with high investment risks. The residents, then, begin the follow-up process that leads to residents investing in their community. The creation of social and economic capital by residents for the benefit of their community is a completely autonomous transaction that is not subject to the paternalism of the state or any other outside force. Nor will it be subject to the dependency that has stifled economic growth within developing neighborhoods.

Legal rights education is the other touchstone of CEDAD. Community leaders believe that a basic understanding of what residents are entitled to under the law is crucial to the initiation of the problem-solving process. In a zone of little code compliance by landlords and no enforcement of codes by the government, assuming residents realize their legal rights is misguided. Learning to access the situation in light of legal rights promotes the empowerment aspect of this problem-solving process. Upon appreciation of their situation, residents are better informed to voice the course of action that they want to take and feel more closely tied to their decision. They learn to identify needs and utilize the partnerships created by CEDAD to achieve an adequate and efficient response.

The community's right to self-determination is preserved through this model. By using the counseling techniques prescribed, the autonomy of the resident is respected, transforming a singular voice into a self-advocating force. The residents are the ultimate beneficiaries of the legal rights education and service projects because of their identity as collaborator. By learning the qualities of self-advocacy as well as how to manage the resources provided by partnerships like CEDAD, residents turn a feeling of hopelessness into a feeling of ownership of the problem as well as the ways in which the problem can be solved.

WHAT THE COMMUNITY LEARNS

Clinics and partnerships such as those being constructed through the efforts of residents of the West Coconut Grove, the students and professors of the University of Miami's Schools of Law and Architecture, and those who have donated their expertise and money, like Legal Services and Greenberg Traurig, are teaching the city of Miami as a whole how to engage in the rebellious vision of the community building process. CEDAD is teaching the community the value of employing the low-income neighborhood residents as crucial collaborators and of centering action on that community's pool of local knowledge.

The clinic serves another communal function as it creates a consciousness for development issues that would otherwise be ignored. By voicing the needs of residents as the residents see them and highlighting inefficiencies in responses by the government, CEDAD is improving the governmental accountability. CEDAD's commitment to ensuring that the benefits ultimately accrue to the residents as evidenced by the work on the community land trust and other anti-gentrification meas-

Photo courtesy of CEDAD

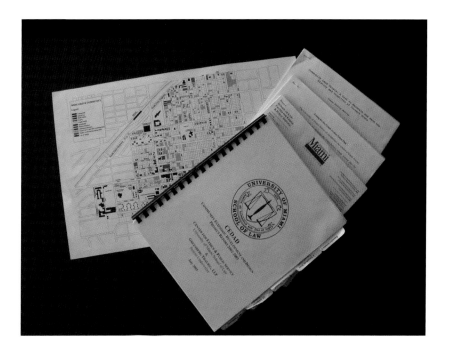

ures sets an example for city policy makers. Municipal equity projects that attack the unequal and unconstitutional allocation and distribution of services and resources across the city neighborhood lines push politicians and agency leaders to act more like scholars and less like political functionaries, an important change for Miami if the growth of the class chasm is to be curbed.

The study and implementation of rebellious vision of problem-solving that empowers those who have been systematically disenfranchised from the workings of the law, creating a more equitable and democratically inclusive development process, is a cause that should be championed by anyone concerned with the future vitality of American cities. If communities are to be families, then it is clinics like CEDAD that will help to bind the ties.

FOOTNOTES

1.   See http://www.census.gov/c2ss/www/Products/Profiles/
2000/index.htm.
2.   Anthony V. Alfieri, (1991) "Reconstructive Poverty Law Practice: Learning Lessons of Client Narrative" in *100 Yale Law Journal* 2107 (1991).
3.   Samina Quraeshi (2002) "The Spirit of Place", in *The Living Traditions of Coconut Grove*, a publication of the University of Miami School of Architecture and INUSE (on file with authors)
4.   See http://www.upenn.edu/ccp/Bibliography/I_Harkavy_ Testimony.html (website accessed: 12/01/04)
5.   Gerald P. Lopez (2004) Shaping Community Problem Solving

Around Community Knowledge, *79 N.Y.U.L.Rev.* 59, 76
6.   *Id.* at 67.
7.   See American Bar Association (1992) *The Report of the Task Force on Law Schools and the Profession: Narrowing the Gap*
8.   John C. Dubin (1998) "Clinical Design for Social Justice Imperatives" in *51 SMU Law Review* 1461, 1465
9.   See Center for Ethics and Public Service University of Miami School of Law (2002), *Community Economic Development and Design Project Report 2000-2002* at 21 (on file with authors).
10.   Anthony V. Alfieri (1991) "Reconstructive Poverty Law Practice: Learning Lessons of Client Narrative", in *100 Yale Law Journal.* 2107, 2120
11.   See Peter Pitegoff (1995) "Law School Initiatives in Housing and Community Development", in *4 B.U. Pub. Int. L.* 275
12.   Anthony Alfieri, (1994) "Practicing Community (Review of Lopez: Rebellious Lawyering", in *107 Harv. L.Rev.* 1747, 1760 (1994).
13.   *Id.* at 1759.
14.   *Id.*
15.   See Robert D. Dinerstein, (1988) "Client-Centered Counseling: Reappraisal and Refinement", in *32 Ariz. L. Rev.* 501
16.   Paul R. Tremblay (1992) "Theoretics of Practice: The Integration of Progressive Thought and Action: Rebellious Lawyering, Regnant Thinking, and Street Level Bureaucracy" in *43 Hastings L.J.* 947, 952
17.   Gerald P. Lopez (2004) "Shaping Community Problem Solving Around Community Knowledge", in *79 N.Y.U. L. Rev.* 59, 114
18.   See generally, American Bar Association (1994) *Findings of the Comprehensive Legal Needs Study*
19.   See generally, (1974) Marc Galanter, "Why the "Haves" Come Out ahead: Speculations on the Limits of Legal Change", in *9 Law and*

LEARNING FROM THE PAST, LOOKING TO THE FUTURE

It is the fundamental truth
of the town, and one that
Americans, for example,
have been loath to accept:
that there can be no peace,
no complete town either,
until communal values
transcend those of individual
competition.

Vincent Scully

The Individual and the Community

Elizabeth Plater-Zyberk
University of Miami School of Architecture

In recent years, social scientists have succeeded in making the case that the wellbeing of the individual relates to the integrity of the family, and that families benefit from the support of an interactive community—the neighborhood. The maxim "It takes a village to raise a child" has become a universal refrain.

Photo: Douglas Robbins

In turn, the sustenance of community requires the commitment of the individual to the common good of one's neighbors. After years of promoting autonomy as a benchmark of mental health, we hear from psychologists that interdependence may be a more fruitful approach to human relations.

One individual's behavior can have a salutatory effect on group comportment—or, conversely, a demoralizing one. In the U.S., we are dealing with the experience of broken families living in broken neighborhoods in declining cities, with the understanding that this threat is posed not only to the well-being of a city but also to our society at large.

This relationship of the individual to the community has a parallel structure in the physical environment. The individual building plays a role in the integrity of the neighborhood, and multiple strong neighborhoods contribute to the prosperity of a city. Cities are now components that comprise metropolitan regions or city–states, which, current economic theory suggests, are the organic increment of economic power and competition.

We are all part of a global community, acknowledging earthly interdependence every time the media announces the growing dimension of the hole in the ozone, or whenever we log onto the Internet. But while the Internet reminds us of the universal scale of community, the building patterns of the last half-century do not necessarily reflect the acknowledged relationship between the built environment and human behavior in daily activities. Rather, they reflect the emphasis on autonomy and separation. In the twentieth century we jettisoned the neighborhood—a compact, pedestrian friendly, mixed-use residential increment of city-making—in favor of the suburban arrangement of separated housing subdivisions, strip shopping and office parks.

Thus we have produced suburban sprawl and urban disinvestment; we have made ourselves automobile-dependent, seeking new places while leaving old places behind; and we have chosen to live as monocultures, separating ourselves by race and wealth and age. Yet we know that a sense of community rooted in commitment to interdependence and the nuances of place is a sustainable social ecology. It is especially important at the beginning and end of our lives when proximity to a support network of caregivers plays a critical role.

Photo: Jennifer Boehm

The physical environment can and should be structured according to immutable principles of mutual benefit, which have been acquired throughout history, such as locating daily needs within walking distance of residence. The neighborhood—a community of place—provides the ideal setting for mutual benefit. This is a place where:

• children can walk to school
• adolescents can engage friends in the socializing process under the watchful eye of neighbors or local business owners who know their parents
• young adults can find small apartments above or next to neighborhood shops
• young couples can purchase small houses and growing families can move into larger houses, rather than leaving the community
• workers can walk or take transit to reach their jobs, parent caretakers and home workers are within a short walk of company on the main street or at a church, and elderly people can find support from caring neighbors nearby.

Historic West Coconut Grove could be such a place. With an identifiable center and boundary, an optimum overall dimension related to convenient walking distance (a half mile across), a mix of housing for all ages and incomes, places to shop and to work, schools, parks and the adjacent Metro-Rail station, the neighborhood is laid out on a grid of interconnected streets that encourages walking and the formation of the informal bonds of community.

Neighborhoods like West Coconut Grove can be clean, safe, satisfying places to grow up and grow old. Their stewardship can change the disposable city syndrome that characterizes much of urban America.

With a new understanding of the structure of community, old places can teach us about making new communities sustainable. These are places where people want to live and work and which people want to maintain and preserve. From communities of place a simple impetus for forming bonds of community can emerge in a time of increasing diversity and mobility. The people who share a place, a neighborhood that is functional and beautiful, and who share the desire to preserve its character and social value, will have to work together.

Protecting and enhancing place can be a powerful, constructive and unifying force for community. A neighborhood that recognizes its unique character and whose residents work together to maintain and enhance it can become a powerful model for a larger increment of society—even a whole city or region.

Photos: Douglas Robbins

Next Steps
The Spirit of Place

Samina Quraeshi
Initiative for Urban and Social Ecology (INUSE)

Photo: Samina Quraeshi

As this collection of histories, portraits and interventions has shown, both community service and university education benefit from being practiced together, especially in a context of local relevance and national precedent. Reimagining West Coconut Grove attempts to weave a portrait of a community in transition. Our efforts in the Grove should be seen as a case study of what can happen when a multidisciplinary approach is taken to the process of community-building. We do not have the answers, but we have learned a lot and have lessons to share from both our successes and our failures.

Many of the changes evident in the target area over the past five years make us proud. But without critical reflection on the assumptions and limitations of the project, our mistakes will be repeated. As all of us have realized from past efforts in rebuilding communities: no one or two approaches can solve a problem. Only with many lenses and tools can the issues that obstruct healthy community life can be observed and, hopefully, ameliorated.

The University of Miami's multidisciplinary effort has looked through the lenses of History, Architecture, Education, Communications, Law, Art, Urban Design and Psychology to develop new ways of seeing the complexities of a neighborhood in need. Meanwhile, partners from within the community have responded with educational, housing and service projects that are beginning to inspire fellow citizens to engage in the process.

By beginning to forge strong new relationships between the university and the community, and within the university itself, however, this experiment has revealed the effectiveness of reaching beyond single projects and unrelated social programs. What has emerged is a holistic perspective on how important it is to envision a neighborhood from many disciplines, to respect all of its unique characteristics, and observe and listen as much as we teach and tell. Through this work we are seeing how a university, when it unleashes its resources, can yield lifelong learning for all of its participants, and carry out research that can be a catalyst for positive change.

Our goal now is to take this patchwork of images, stories, buildings and spaces and create a more cohesive strategy for identifying and implementing community goals and revitalizing this and other historic neighborhoods.

BUILDING COMMUNITY THROUGH UNIVERSITY PARTNERSHIPS

Community is about individuals who care. In a well-functioning community everyone is welcome. Community also remains the basic context through which people contribute their talents to society: it is only through a network of relationships that collective capacity can be built.

If the last half-century has taught community activists anything, it is that conventional community-development and social-service programs are powerless to stem the deterioration of the social and neighborhood fabric. Such programs translate needs into deficiencies, and then formulate "one-size-fits-all" responses that deny the special circumstances surrounding each human problem. Caught in the confusion between real and perceived needs, people lose faith in the very institutions whose purpose is to help them.

The Initiative for Urban and Social Ecology (INUSE) is one new vision for building our society — family by family, block by block. Through foresight, imagination and design, we believe communities and families can grow together — the spirit of place nourishing strong families that, in turn, cohere into sound communities.

Central to our approach is the idea that building and renovating livable communities happens through the conscious acts of design. By engaging families and residents with their environment, we can create places that people care about, take pride in, and fight to protect.

By applying our imagination and creativity, we can reestablish a sense of community that will endure, and that people and businesses will reinvest in, generation after generation.

But this approach betrays a fundamental bias that limits the transformative potential of our model. INUSE was framed as an interdisciplinary

effort from the start, but it was developed from within a design pedagogy. As we have seen in this volume, the design framework led to some positive steps. Projects have included designing and building affordable homes on infill sites, renovating commercial properties, facilitating neighborhood planning for a new community school and health facility, identifying discrepancies in zoning and planning that discourage investment and working with the City and county to rectify them, holding charrettes, facilitating legal assistance for neighborhood residents, and creating a Community Resource Center that coordinates existing and new community improvement efforts, and establishing a community-run collaborative.

But INUSE also reflects the mandate of the Henry R. Luce Professor in Family and Community at the University of Miami. The Luce Professorship was created to foster an interdisciplinary program of research, education and outreach in support of the people, places and processes needed to create and sustain family-centered communities. This interdisciplinary program brings together students and faculty members from six different university departments and schools to work on research, education, and outreach for the neighborhood. In total, 272 students and 40 faculty members to date have been involved in this effort to catalyze long-term change in this neighborhood and equip residents with the knowledge and skills to assume responsibility for their community. Each semester, more students become involved. Through their engagement in academically based community service, the students are enhancing both their minds and hearts, and gaining "real world" experience in which they can apply their academic knowledge.

But there was a far more important barrier to cross than the segmentation of knowledge into academic fields of expertise. To be sure, operating between disciplinary traditions has required innovation as well as patience. But a far greater challenge was in creating a sustainable collaborative relationship between the university and the community. We assumed that the goals of both stakeholders would be the same.

Across the country, universities are becoming increasingly aware that existing traditions of self-directed research and teaching were insufficient in addressing the present needs of society. In Miami, the physical and social needs of neighborhoods like West Coconut Grove are urgent, complex, and interconnected. Clearly, the city can benefit greatly from the university's expertise and "cultural capital." For its part, the university can become a better neighbor, and it can benefit programmatically, from tying research activities to improvements in the quality of life in real time.

But seeking to stem processes of social decomposition requires a comprehensive, nuanced approach to social, economic and physical renaissance. And this rebirth is only possible by restoring a strong fabric of both social processes and physical settings that will help families evolve out of isolation into community.

Face-to-face with social and economic inequity in West Coconut Grove, we have tried to open our eyes to the physical reality of place and the spirit of the people who live there. In a realistic rather than nostalgic light, we have tried to discover what exists (and rediscover what once existed). Only from such a foundation can we hope to envision what might be.

LANGUAGE, INTENT AND POWER

"Urban regeneration," "inner-city revitalization," "comprehensive redevelopment," "cultural preservation," "community building." We hear many names these days for a diverse set of policy strategies and social phenomena that have the same vague themes, and that are built on a similar commitment to improving the quality of life in a community. Often these terms are used interchangeably, but it is also important to engage this language directly and to unpack the political agendas inherent in each term.

If one examines these words more closely, one can see how "regeneration" involves a metaphor from the natural world — as in the growth of a new tail. "Revitalization" shares such connotations of renewal; but it

also implies a condition of death that can only be redressed through the (re)infusion of new life. "Redevelopment" reminds us of the dark postwar chapters in American urban history. It evokes the materiality of concrete more than the essence of social vigor. "Cultural preservation" suggests an elitist agenda bent on exorcising an assumed mass irrationality symptomatic of the public impulse toward homogeneity. Finally, "community-building" essentializes cohesive social networks (to the exclusion of other infrastructural forms) as the conceptual building blocks of renaissance.

None of these strategies is unproblematic from the point of view of a new university/community initiative. Nor could they ever be. Despite all our inclusive rhetoric of "partnership" and "collaboration," an inevitable disparity exists between university and community. Thus, our work begs a number of questions:

How can a partnership between the university and the community be managed so that the community leads, or at least is not overwhelmed by academic initiative?

How could this new partnership engage the resources necessary to implement the evolving goals?

How would the efforts ensure that the ultimate benefits accrue to the community and its residents and in particular that potential improvements do not displace residents and businesses?

How can the community be organized as a unified and effective force to be best able to take full advantage of the attention bestowed by its university partners?
How can the community develop the social capacity to continue community-building and enhancement as an ongoing aspect of its future?

In practical terms, we have tried to address this divide between university and community by listening. We have set out to get to know the community, mapping its assets and understanding the existing community organizations before attempting to arrive at any vision or implement any plan.

From the other side of the table, a primary motivator is the potential for

Photo: Richard Shepard

large-scale economic change. But we have also tried to be clear about our principles. For us, creating a sense of place means restoring a belief in progress. And by "progress," we mean access to affordable housing, the restoration of a sense of history, the creation of community identity, and the establishment of the proper climate for reinvestment.

Such negotiations are clearly very difficult. And the failure to attend to such discussions only leads to the breakdown of civic life, as communities become more fragmented and individual lives more privatized.

THE ROLE OF EXPERTISE

Any long-term project forces one to confront assumptions. My personal training, as a designer and artist, has led me to look into my past as inspiration for future projects, most of which involved identifying some essence or fragment of personal history and repositioning it as a cairn for emotional way-finding in the future.

In a similar way, much new urban-design thought, specifically the New Urbanism movement, has put a premium on pedestrian access as a vital component of sustainable and livable communities. Such a view is clearly derived from socially constructed memories of small-town living, but I do not see such constructions as deterministic. Rather, I see them as metaphors guiding the work of experts who have more at stake in the process of community-building than do developers out to maximize their return on investment.

Yet an outsider can never truly understand the patterns and relationships that constrain or foment change. We came to West Coconut Grove wielding the cultural power of the academic, the designer, the "expert." But expertise, if not continuously challenged for its relevance and mode of application, can become another vehicle for silencing the aspirations it was meant to emancipate.

Expertise also does not guarantee success. Armed with precedents of urban renewal, theories to underpin our beliefs, and even knowledge of the history of the community, we have still found that an important piece of the puzzle remains elusive.

The history of the West Grove and its inhabitants is rich, and we were so eager to leverage it as a tool for community building that we didn't pause to critically investigate what that history signifies to the community's inhabitants. Yet, our work has been heavily biased towards the notion that the history of the neighborhood could be a positive and creative force toward fashioning a sense of community.

I still believe it can, but not without critical insight into the complex politics of what history signifies. This process is inherently political, because it seeks to reclaim a shared sense of collective identity, and collective identity is the basis of political community.
In West Coconut Grove we have had to address what happens if what unites a group of people is the trauma of history, not the pride of place it is supposed to infuse into the neighborhood. How, then, should we, as community builders, constructively engage with the past?

THE PROBLEM OF PRESERVATION

In the West Grove neighborhood, a preservationist impulse at first loomed large in our conceptualizations of the project. But as the scope widened, recurring questions began to bother us: preservation by whom? For whom? Community building is a new and interdisciplinary field, and part of its challenge is in rethinking the deterministic (and paternalistic) urbanism of much of the twentieth century.

The politics of preservation are complex, and they hinge on the contest between a high idealism that would conserve the past in static form and a crass consumerism that would use it for present commercial purposes. While many preservation interests are indigenous to a community, both these forces normally act on it from the outside. And, a cultural divide often follows between those members of the community for whom the preservation furthers a cultural agenda and those for whom it furthers an economic agenda.

Identifying patterns is the basis of any scholarly research. And precedents are constantly cited as proof of the viability of any initiative. Yet, as much as models are necessary to implement a vision, no easy model for rebuilding a lost sense of community has yet been successfully devised. We need a new model, one that can engage the pluralism of a community's dreams for its future, and not only its occasionally suspect memories and history.

Each neighborhood has its own biology and chemistry and history of alliances or feuds. And over the history of West Coconut Grove as a community there have been major shifts— racial, ethnic, economic and cultural — that correspond to the sense of identity and place of the people who live there. Rebuilding what once was may not be what is best for the future.

LESSONS FROM THE WEST GROVE

By listening to the people of West Coconut Grove one discovers that "community" is not a static concept. Indeed, the assumption that the community is, or was once, whole and cohesive contradicts the historic record and contemporary realities.

In this regard we must guard against our perceptions becoming tainted by nostalgia for an idealized past that never existed, and has therefore not been lost. Nostalgia helps bring back happy memories to those who have a past in a place, but it may not be best for those who see a different future, and increasingly, West Coconut Grove is not so much a Bahamian-American community as it is a poor community.

In her penetrating study of nostalgia, Svetlana Boym wrote of the spatial dimension of nostalgia. The longing (algia in Greek) is for one's home (nostos), a home that either no longer exists or may in fact have never existed . In this sense, nostalgia has been a common motivator of diasporic communities. Yet, critics have often found fault with nostalgia's undue prevalence in New Urbanism and neoliberalism.

At the same time, community has always been a collection of individuals, sometimes supporting, sometimes in conflict with one another, and of social structures and institutions that evolve along with the needs of people and the greater forces surrounding them. And while it may still be possible for members of an ethnic group to feel bound together by common origin, custom, religion or language, and to feel different from other groups, larger social forces make it less likely than ever that such a cultural enclave can constitute a community. Traditional ethnic communities, like West Grove, are changing into areas defined more by levels of education, income and access to jobs, than by cultural identity.

The diffusion of people, jobs and resources out of West Grove has placed enormous financial and social burdens on this older urban neighborhood. As the more educated and well-to-do members of the community leave an ethnic enclave, the social fabric frays. But I believe nostalgia can be a powerful tool when separated from its most overly sentimental and reactionary proclivities. And its use as part of an urban renewal strategy in the West Grove is totally commensurate with the need to generate a new value structure in a community that has lost touch with its history.

But at the same time INUSE's West Coconut Grove project demonstrates first-hand that we must reimagine community less in terms of static racial or ethnic identities and more by the shared goals of diverse residents, working together and using their individual assets and collective power to promote cohesion and foster change. We need to learn from the neighborhoods' families, as they adapt to the vagaries of birth, death, marriage and other life changes. Under pressure, families either break down or forge stronger connections across ethnic, cultural, religious, social and economic bounds. Communities must learn the same lesson of adaptation to reimagine their own identities through interethnic connections.

INUSE IN PROSPECT

The INUSE initiative comes at a critical time, when poor neighborhoods across the country are confronted with a myriad of social, economic and infrastructural problems. Many communities struggle with such interrelated problems as building an economic base, reducing substance abuse, addressing mental health problems, decreasing welfare rolls, and bolstering employment opportunities. As our work shows, it is no longer sufficient or even feasible to take simple actions like knocking down and replacing buildings, or to address single issues in isolation.

INUSE has played a pivotal role in mediating among community organizations, religious groups and political agencies in efforts to promote pride and mobilize resources. It has demonstrated how the university can be a good neighbor by focusing on small-scale goals that add up to larger change. From legal-aid and small-business clinics to plans for the School of Medicine to allow better access to health and human services, the University of Miami is in position to be a stabilizing influence.

But INUSE has also provided a venue for learning. At the heart of the INUSE program are dedicated University of Miami students who become change agents/problem solvers. Among other critical "living" skills, students learn to meet and interact with community decision-makers; collaborate with policy-makers in the city, country and state government; apply cross-disciplinary theory to practice; experience the difficulty and satisfaction of completing real work; participate in an ethnically and socially diverse group setting.

The University of Miami is not alone. Several universities across the country are initiating community-based programs that are similar to INUSE. INUSE has built upon the lessons of like-minded efforts to involve an even broader range of university disciplines, such as behavioral sciences, economic counseling and legal aid. Through these partnerships, University of Miami students not only study a neighborhood from multiple perspectives but also contribute to real-life solutions with an impact beyond the confines of the academic semester. INUSE helps students understand and foster the crucial connections between learning and action, theory and practice, and education and citizenship.

We feel this effort to immerse the formal education process in real places in real time is a promising way to understand families and community and to enhance civic life. And it allows students to better relate academic disciplines such as history, art, architecture and behavioral psychology to their own communities.

INUSE will continue to expand by involving students and faculty from additional disciplines, particularly those that will help the West Grove address its economic difficulties. To thrive socially, a community and its residents must thrive economically, and for that to happen, its members must have full access to business and professional training, to development and investment opportunities, and to the technologies that sustain successful enterprises.

INUSE is also seeking to expand its role locally and nationally by sponsoring innovative projects in other Miami communities; sponsoring outstanding national mentors to visit and participate in the INUSE program; sponsoring a national leadership conference for universities, communities and cities to explore the INUSE model. We see these projects and centers as part of a growing family of University-led initiatives to engage with their communities. But the potential of institutional collaborations must extend beyond this model. Institutions of commerce, industry, faith and local government, each of which has its own tradition of community service, must coordinate efforts in new ways. Individuals must continue to maintain the momentum of positive change by constantly renewing their commitment to grass-roots projects.

But as these efforts expand, we must never lose sight of why we build community and what community means. Community is about individuals who care. In a well-functioning community everyone is welcome. Community also remains the basic context through which people contribute their talents to society: it is only through a network of relationships that collective capacity can be built.

The history of communities and families often run in tandem. A sense of community – whether on an inner-city block or at a lonesome country crossroads — emerges initially from a sense of families at home, sharing common bonds and interests, building the infrastructures necessary to protect from want and filling the needs of faith, sustenance and ambition. Upon such common foundations of shelter, sustenance, love and companionship communities may rise and fall through time. But like great families, great communities must also adapt to flourish: they must be innovative in responding to social and cultural change, and they must accommodate new members for growth, economic strength, and diversity.

We invite the participation of everybody concerned with the future of communities, the American city, and a civil society to join our efforts in the pragmatic philosophy and practice of learning through service.

The design of places is about finding - and forging relationships.
Relationships between:
                        people and things
                                people and buildings
buildings and landscape
                        landscape and resources
                                landscape and institutions
institutions and process
                        process and people
                                people and community.
                                        Donlyn Lyndon

Photo: Douglas Robbins

The Second Wave of Engagement: Learning From West Coconut Grove

David Scobey, Director, Arts of Citizenship Program
Taubman College of Architecture University of Michigan

Re-Imagining West Coconut Grove is at once the record, the product, and (one hopes) the inaugural chapter of a sustained partnership between the University of Miami and the economically poor, historically rich neighborhood bordering its campus. The University's participation was led by the Initiative for Urban and Social Ecology and INUSE's director Samina Quraeshi, the Henry R. Luce Professor in Family and Community; it included faculty and students from not only architecture and urban planning (INUSE's institutional home), but also law, public health, history, art, and other disciplines. West Coconut Grove collaborators included the Coconut Grove Local Development Corporation, members of tenant associations and other grass-roots groups, educators, artists, activists, and community historians; many residents contributed their memories of the neighborhood's past, their visions for its future, and their views on its current needs and resources. The sheer extent of the partnership, on both sides of the town/gown boundary, is impressively showcased here. We learn about master plans, architectural projects, and home building efforts; oral history, public art, and photo-documentary projects; legal, health, and other programs that help to meet the neighborhood's pressing needs. An outside observer can only admire the multi-stranded, interdisciplinary weave of the West Coconut Grove partnership.

This volume documents five years of dynamic work. And yet it feels like a first installment, Part One of a collaboration that holds the potential to be both physically and intellectually ground-breaking. Some of the initiatives described here (the master planning, oral history collection) have been brought close to closure; others (home construction, photo-essays, legal clinics) are well-begun; still others are envisioned but remain undone. One can only hope that the University of Miami renews its commitment to the neighborhood and its own scholars' and students' engagement. Yet whatever its future, the West Coconut Grove partnership already represents a significant chapter in a larger story, an unfolding saga of civic renewal and intellectual engagement within American higher education. Its roots and its implications stretch far beyond Coconut Grove. Indeed the project makes clear just how cosmopolitan such local work can be.

The formation of INUSE within the University of Miami's College of Architecture in the late 1990s coincided with the acceleration of a twenty-year campaign for civic engagement and community collaboration in the American academy. Concerned that the expansion, expense, complexity, and perceived arrogance of colleges and universities had undermined their effectiveness and legitimacy, administrators and faculty sought to repair the frayed compact between higher education and the larger society. The first fruit of that effort was the proliferation of service learning across American campuses. Indeed the 1986 founding of Campus Compact, a national consortium to support academic service learning, can be said to have launched the movement for civic engagement. Notwithstanding its pedagogical vibrancy, however, service learning often remained marginal to curricular and faculty priorities, a respected adjunct to the core educational mission of most institutions. Beginning in the mid-1990s, faculty, staff, and academic leaders, both within and without the service learning movement, responded with new models of engagement. They sought to create sustained university-community partnerships that set and met goals collaboratively, projects that would fully integrate community practice